THE BASILICA OF TORCELLO AND SANTA FOSCA'S

Texts of the priest Antonio Niero

Published by KINA ITALIA

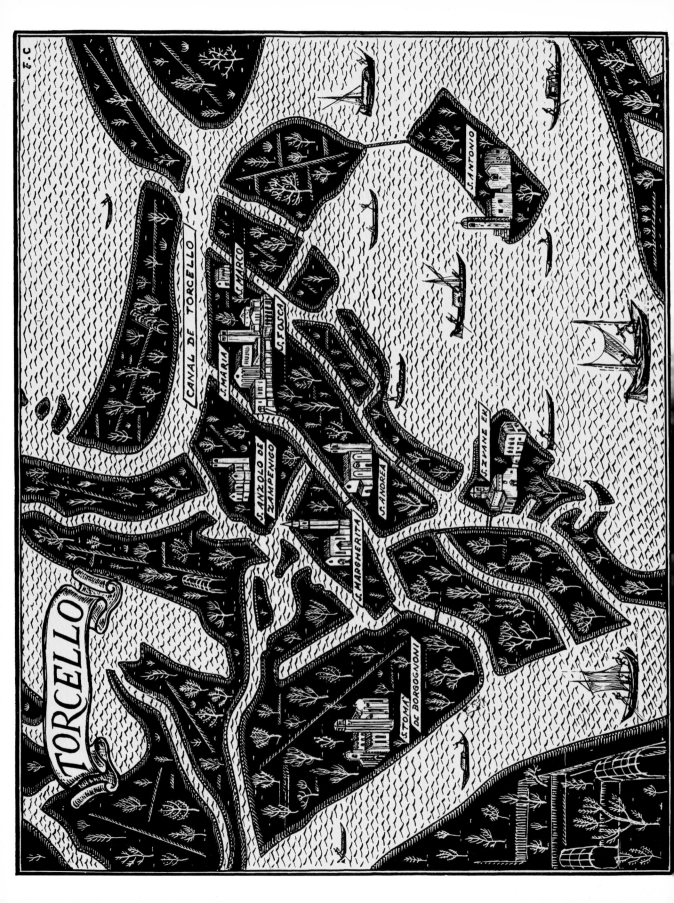

Dear reader,

Many people have written on Torcello and its interesting monuments. Prof. Antonio Niero, well versed in the matter, offers you a historical, artistic guide of S. Maria Assunta's Basilica, a monument famous for its byzantine mosaics and of S. Fosca's church, a characteristic greek-byzantine building.

These wonderful antiques of the ancient town, now formed by a few houses with few inhabitants owing to historical and natural events, are a witness of the grandeur of the glorious, splendid past of Torcello, rich in art and faith.

We present it to you, hoping to please you, but our best thaks are for the author and Marzari Co. which printed it.

May you get the wonderful message these works communicate from these pages.

THE EDITOR

The Basilica and S. Fosca's

By tradition, Torcello (Torcellum) derives its name from one of the ancient gates of the roman town of Altino, which stood in front of the present Torcello, like a small defence tower. As the same name is present in some places of the plain of the Po, it is more probable that also in the lagoon we have to go back to a pre-roman origin, with a meaning of lagoon geography, i.e. a place emerged among the marshes, as the other ancient denomination *Dorceum* can confirm. It was probably inhabited during the roman epoch; at least in the imperial time when some Villas of Altino, remembered by Marziale's famous lines (died in 102), might have been built. In fact owing to the excavations made by the Polish archaeological mission in 1961-62, they ascertained the presence of a roman installation, during the first and second cent. A.C., with traces of houses. During the Vth cent. this installation was destroyed by the adverse geographic conditions; perhaps a strong, rough sea, connected with the disorder of the venetian river regimes submerged everything. In the VIth, VIIth cent. there are new traces of a repopulating, documented by the ruins of a circular furnace, used for the glass manufacture and other activities of bronze and furnishings. But we have got some more important documents. The famous epigraphic inscription, found in the cathedral and kept there, remembers that the Basilica consecrated to Maria, Mother of God was built in 639 for account of Isaac, the exarch of Ravenna; the bishop was perhaps Mauro. It is not worth arguing if this inscription refers to Torcello as scholars affirm, or to Cittanova Eracleiana, near the present Eraclea. It is probable the bishop Mauro led here his faithful running away from Altino, where the Longobards' pressure was intensifying. The same dedication to God's Mother (Theotócos) meant an affirmation of catholic faith against the Arian Longobard likings and the devotedness to the emperor Eraclio, crier of the devotion to God's Mother.

We don't know the plan of this primitive cathedral, Perhaps, it stood on the area of the present one, rebuilt in 1008, with a central apse, included into a perimetric wall, and two rudimentary small apses, according to the upper Adriatic typical lagoon scheme . At the beginning of the XVIIIth cent. the bishop Adeodato I completed the building adorning it with marble decorations, as the chronicler Giovanni Diacono, a well informed source, wrote at the end of the XXth cent. Other important works were made by the bishop Adeodato II (864-867); the prolongation of the central apse beyond the perimetric wall, the enlargement of the two small side apses, of the crypt and the porch before the facade. About 1000 the bishop Orso Orseolo, the son of the Doge Pietro Orseolo II, a true follower of his family's tradition, who had taken an interest in holy buildings (his grandfather, the Doge Orseolo I, the Saint, had rebuilt S. Marco's), gave the basilica the present shape, by heightening the central nave, opening some windows in the west wall and the facade and by heightening the floor and building new columns and the ciborium on the altar, later demolished. He erected the majestic bell tower, too. So we remember three buildings of Torcello cathedral: the first in 639 (of which it remains only the low part of the facade, completed at the end of the cent.); the second in 864-867, due to the bishop Adeodato II of which it remains some present elements; the third, wanted by the bishop Orso Orseolo, about 1008, still showing itself in the superb architectonic greatness. During the following centuries many other elements adorned it; by the end of 1100 and the beginning of 1200 they probably built the present mosaics, the central apse, the back facade, and the right apse and by the end of 1200 the silver altar-piece, now gone to ruin and placed in the near museum and in the XIII cent. the plutei of the three door wall (iconostasi) coming from S. Marco's Basilica, according to a recent hypothesis. In 1423, under the bishop Pietro Nani, there was a general restoration of the basilica and the present pictures of the partition wall were probably painted by Zanino di Pietro in this occasion. There were other restorations in 1646, when a thunderbolt damaged the cathedral, the bell tower and the episcopate, seriously, and other works of consolidation in 1821 and 1827 according to the emperor of Austria, Francesco Primo's will and finally from 1929-39 the two buildings, the Cathedral and S. Fosca, were brought again to their primary lines, ridding them of baroque superstructures. In fact, after the Council of Trente they inserted the typical devotions of that time, such as the altar of S. Liberale, of Assunta, with an altar-piece of Tintoretto, on the left; the Innocents' altar with an altar-piece of Veronese and S. Teonisto's, on the right; the high altar, erected in 1629 according to the projects of Baldassare Longhena and demolished in 1929 to build the present one. The ciborium was destroyed in 1629; the silver altar-piece was put on the partition wall and S. Eliodoro's urn was put over the altar, supported by angelic children's figures (perhaps by Moli) with two angels on the sides, of the school of Longhena and a statue of the Saint, which was replaced by S. Lorenzo Giustiniani's during the XVIIIth cent. The two altars of the side small apses were added in the XIXth cent. Torcello lost its importance as episcopal see and title in 1818 for it was joined to the patriarchate of Venice, it depends upon now, and keeps only the dean title consecrated to S. Maria Assunta (perhaps after 1100); its inhabitants are only one hundred, the glorious rest of one of the most ancient lagoon markets before 1000, celebrated by Costantino Porfirogenito, emperor of Bisanzio, but declined when its activities were gradually absorbed by the rising Venice.

▶
1 - The Isle of Torcello in its lagoon

The Basilica

THE BAPTISTERY

In front of the cathedral there are the remains of the baptistery. It was probably a circular plan building, with an octogonal colonnade inside, forming an annular corridor; in the middle, under a vault, there was the basin for the baptism dipping, administered according to the ancient liturgy at Easter night and whit Sunday one.

We can still see two big niches near the central door, which perhaps contained two altars, the marble threshold, the bases of the columns and traces of painted plaster and the side door. Its plan has no comparison with similar buildings in the Adriatic, but we must go back to Salona of to Siria. Anyhow the plan is typically roman with byzantine annotations, noticeable in the two large side niches, that you can see also in S. Donato of Zara and after 1000, in the roman Cathedral at Iesolo. It is placed before the central door with an evident liturgical introduction function of the catechumens and new christians to the Cathedral. It goes back to the VIIth cent.

THE BASILICA

The present building, i.e. the Orseolo's of 1008, 50 m. long and 21 m. large has three aisles with a heightened central facade, three doors and a front portico of the IXth cent. leaning against the baptistery. It is supported by six round and square columns and opens partly in a full sail vault and partly lean-to roof. In earlier times the colonnade included only four columns; two on the right and two on the left of the baptistery, in the XIVth cent. the woody trusses were modified in the buttress present one, and during the XVth cent. they added two columns on the right side, which joined the porch with the one of the near martyrium of S. Fosca, forming a unitary whole; later, on the left side they added a prolongation in relation to the entrance to the Schola Episcopalis (a room of the brotherhood, with some remains of frescoes). Among the three doors, the jamb of the main entrance decorated with reliefs, deserve a particular attention; on the right there are bunches of grapes, rosettes, and a candelabrum floral interlacing of the period of Orseolo; adove a vine-shoot with grapes and vine-leaves of a previous period, perhaps of the IXth cent. and on the left, geometrical volutes with crosslets, of the period of Orseolo. On the wall there are two remains of a pluteus, perhaps of the IXth cent., and the last door on the left lets in the storehouses added in the XVIth cent. On the right there is a neoclassic Crucifixion of little value; a memorial tablet in honour of Francesco Primo, emperor of Austria, who, thanks to

2 - Sight from the plane of the Basilica of Torcello and S. Fosca

Pyrker (1821-1827), the Patriarch of Venice began the restoration of S. Fosca's Cathedral and the bell tower.

Above the portico there is the brick principal facade, divided into six pillars cut horizontally a little above the connection of the two small side aisles perhaps where the prospect of the IXth cent. ended, creating the illusion of a gallery; it is a whole of Ravenna taste where the wall has a decorative function, getting, in conseguence a sense of brightness due to the grazing shaking of light, which forms some shade plays, according to Bettini's subtle interpretation. Correspondently with the fourth and the fifth pillar there are, above, two bull's eye small windows, built by the Orseolo in 1008 for practical purposes. These ones and the two windows supported by centrings of the second and fifth pillar, opened already in the IXth cent, were closed later, because of the mosaic of the inside wall. You can see the same windows supported by centrings in the two fronts of the small side aisles, built along all the space of the pillars and later blinded. It is possible to remark the persistence of the symbolic motive based on the value of three, the holy number, with reference to the Trinity. Adove, near the typanum there is Pietro Nani, the local bishop's coat of arms, in memory of the restorations of the Cathedral in 1423.

THE INSIDE

You enter the Cathedral through a side door (the remains of two rosette and plait plutei perhaps of the IXth cent. are driven in the wall, while the two inscriptions remembering the church consecration feast are of the XVIth cent.) and feel pervaded by the solemnity of the whole. The light falling through the ten side windows of the central nave, open only on the south part both for a greater lighting and in defence of North cold winds, wherefore the North side has a continued wall, determine, in the colour decomposition of the wall bricks and the reflections of the floor mosaic, an effect of space division of lagoon taste. If there were not the chains amid the columns, a byzantine reminiscence, due already in the period of Orseolo, to technical necessities, to withstand the wall disbanding caused by the ground, according to a rule, frequent in the roman-gothic Venetian churches, the whole would certainly recall S. Apollinare Nuovo in Ravenna. They perhaps wanted to cover the walls of the central nave with mosaics to join the apse and the entrance, but they probably lacked money. The central nave is separated from the side aisles by nine greek marble columns, on each side, with veinings caused by weather and climate; between the seventh and the ninth there is the presbytery, according to a paleochristian, upper Adriatic proceeding that may be found in S. Tommaso di Pola's, too. Almost all the columns are the bishop Orseolo's work, who in part used pre-existing elements; the corinthian capitals are composed in double turn of soft acanthus supporting a low capital and the arches, bordered red according to a lagoon taste. The second and the sixth right capitals are vine-twig and ovule crown ones (VIth cent.), used in the rebuilding of 1008; while the five capitals near the apse are of the Xth cent; The large, present floor, Orseolo's work, is 30 cm. higher than the one of the IXth cent., worked in white-black small cubes and divided into squares as we can see from the excavations of 1939; on the contrary, the present one develops, in the presbitery, in a pretious, geometric play realized in the XIIIth cent. perhaps coeval of the entrance wall mosaics. On the walls of the right small aisle there are two altars; the first of the second part of the XVIth cent. with « The Massacre of the Innocents » a painting of the school of Veronese; the second in a fine polychrome wood intaglio of Paolo Campsa (at the beginning of the XVIIth cent.) modified by Antonio de Poris, shows the bishop Teonisto, the ancient patron of Altino, in the middle; on its sides there are S.

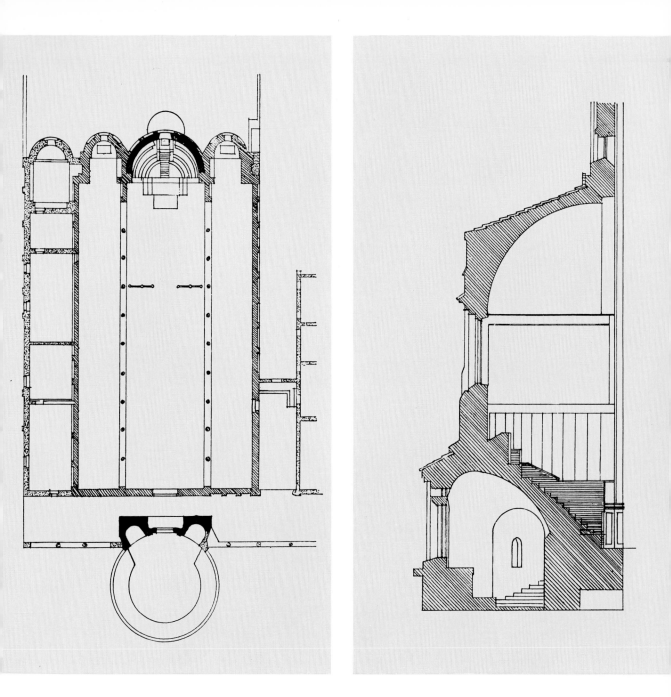

THE PLAN OF THE CATHEDRAL WITH THREE
AISLES AND THE APSE IN FRONT OF THE BAPTI-
STERY.
The walls marked in black colour belong to the first con-
struction of the VII century. The remainders to the fol-
lowing rebuildings.

THE CENTRAL APSE OF THE CATHEDRAL IN
VERTICAL SECTION, WITH THE CRYPTE BELOW,
OBTAINED UNDER THE PRESBYTERIAL EXEDRA.

3 - The inside of the Cathedral seen from the central nave after• the remaking in 1008, under the Bishop Orso Orseolo

▶ *4/5 - Two details of the floor of the Cathedral of the XIth cent.*

12

3

4/5

Antonio and S. Nicola di Bari; above, the Annunciation in reliefs; in the middle there are scenes of the Saint's martyrdom (his preaching and beheading) below, there are the Adoration of the Magi and the Circumcision. Near the entrance small door there is the Madonna with the Child, of a roman master of the XIIIth cent. Near the presbitery there are the bishop Paolo di Altino's tombstone and the partition wall with the holy door in the middle of it, obtained by three small columns half closed by the precious marble plutei and supporting the scenes of the twelve Apostles with the Virgin, attributed by Roberto Longhi to Zanino di Pietro (1423) who worked in Venice at the beginnings of the XVth cent. On the plutei there are two young lions near a tree, marshy ducks pecking the green and two hares playing on the ground; six convolvulus are on the upper part. Two peacocks are catching some grapes, in a vase supported by a tall column, on a ground of curled up and closed leaf vine-tendrils. Some scholars have lately put forth the hypothesis these plutei belonged to the building of the present S. Marco's, moved here, to Torcello, when during the XIIIth cent. they rebuilt the partition wall in S. Marco, in the present shape. The executive preciosity of the whole, obtained by using the drill, with an evident reference to the ivory techniques, and to the same Bisanzio, from where they suppose the creator had arrived, is very noticeable.

The twelve Apostles of the partition wall are: on the right S. Paolo, S. Bartolomeo, S. Giacomo Maggiore, illegible, S. Filippo, S. Giacomo Minore, on the left, S. Pietro, S. Andrea, illegible, and S. Simone, illegible. On the left there is the pulpit, of the XI and XIIth cent. near the presbytery and the aisle of the congregation. Like the ones of Grado and S. Marco, it stands on the right of the altar.

According to Lorenzetti the present arrangement of the pulpit is not the original one, but a following change. At the time of Orseolo there were two pulpits; one on the right side of the choir to read the epistle and one on the left side for the Gospel with double ladder to reach them.

Perhaps, when in 1200 they modified the plutei, employing the present ones, the two pulpits were blended in the present shape, cutting and sawing the decorative marble plates. The first, supported by a polygonal small column used for the epistle the second, with a richer decoration for the Gospel, rests on four columns according to the west scheme; the platform is formed of polychrome marbles and column parapets to let the congregation see the choir and the clergy; around the choir-stand, standing on a small column, there are some human small heads acting as a decorative and a support. The marble plate, protecting the entrance steps on the side of the aisle, has a central floral motive framed by a dentil and tress bundle of the same style and work of the plutei. The huge woody crucifix of the XVth cent. with a rung cross rises on the perpendicular chain of the partition wall.

When you enter the presbytery you see the woody, felze inlaid choir stalls of the clergy, of the XVth cent., the mosaic floor and the right venetian-byzantine plutei (XIth cent.) with a vine rich in leaves and bunches pecked by four gulls; the first on the left represents the pagan myth of Issione, sentenced to death in the XIth cent. the present altar was rebuilt because of the restorations in 1939 on a primitive scheme with different materials found during the works; the altar slab is formed of thick greek marble. Once, in its place, there was a huge baroque building, erected in 1629. In front of it, defended by a lattice, there is the grave of the martyr or *fenestrella confessionis*, protecting a roman sarcophagus of the IInd-IIIrd cent. B.C., brought from Altino by the refuges in 639, keeping the remains of S. Eliodoro, the bishop of Altino, S. Girolamo's friend.

14

6 - *Detail of the partition wall - XV th cent.*

7 - *The « Pluteus of the Peacoks » - A Venetian-Byzantine relief which represents two peacocks drinking at the source of Eternal Life - XIth cent.*

8 - *The « Pluteus of the Lions ». A Venetian-Bizantine relief of the XIth cent. which forms, as the previous one, a parapet in the partition wall of the Cathedral*

7

8

9 - *A woody Crucifix of the XIth cent.*

10 - *The Pulpit of the Cathedral, near the partition wall, placed here and renewed in the XII-XIIIth cent.*

▶ 11 - *The mosaic of the central Apse. In the middle of the golden conch there is the Virgin with the Blessing Child; below there are twelve Apostles; over the triumphal arch the Annunciation - XIIth-XIIIth cent.*

Behind the altar there is the apse basin characterized by several elements; first of all the bishop's throne, rising above six circular flights of stairs. Ten steps, with a clear call to the Ten Commandments lead to it. The system of leaning the episcopal throne against the bottom apse is still of the Upper Adriatic, as it is present in S. Maria delle Grazie in Grado of the Vth cent. as working out of a west or Syriac system and in S. Irene's church in Costantinopoli. The clergy placed themselves on the side steps, in the course of solemn rites or councils, according to the liturgic order; deacons, subdeacons acolyte exorcists, door-keepers, lectors. From the throne the cathedral appears much wider and longer; from there the bishop had the impression of being really the helmsman of his people and island. On the right side there are some inscriptions, one in honour of the bishop Marco Zeno in remembrance of the removal of the holy bodies; on the left there is an inscription of 629, a precious document on the history of Torcello and the lagoons.

Above the steps and the throne there was a series of frescoes, come to light during the restorations of 1939, of benedectine style, near the ones of the crypt of Aquileia, dealing with the subject of the Saints near Christ. Perhaps they were covered with a series of big plates in the XIIth cent. In the middle, perpendiculary on the episcopal throne there is the modern remaking mosaic of S. Eliodoro, the ancient patron of Torcello diocese, he who joins the militant church with the triumphant one, according the medieval canonic conception. In fact above him it goes on a paradisiac procession of the Apostles, ending in the hieratic, beautiful figure of God's mother. These mosaics were remade, for the most part, at the end of last cent; but they still keep an undoubted value. The Apostles proceed, in alternate symmetry in the low folds of the priestly planet, on a meadow where the five or six flower red weeds, a typical plant of the lagoon prairies, bloom.

They are dressed like the Apostles of Ravenna, each of them with his own symbol, divided six by six with S. Paolo, Matteo, Andrea, Giacomo, Mattia, Filippo, on the right and S. Pietro, Giovanni, Giacomo maggiore, Bartolomeo, Taddeo; Tommaso on the left.

The centre is occupied by the east small window, symbol of Crist *oriens ex alto* and the Virgin, east door in the prophet Ezechiele's opinion, in fact the explanation *porta salutis* coincides with the side of the window. Above, it runs, within a fascia, the invocation in Leonine verse inspired to S. Bernardo from Chiaravalle's doctrine of the Blessed Virgin: *Formula virtutis, maris astrum, porta salutis, prole Maria levat, quas coniunge subdidit Eva.* (Mary, Formula of virtue, Sea star, Salvation door, sets free, with her Son, those whom Eva and Adam reduced to sin.) The sublime figure of God's Mother, Móter Then, as the abbreviation in greek says, prevails in the apse basin within concentric zones of gilt mosaic narrowing slowly on high. According to the byzantine scheme of the Odegetria, she comes down gliding gently from the sky in the revelation of the Divinity. It rests on the worship footstool, decorated with twelve gems, while the right knee scarcely reveals the descent movement.

She is dressed like a queen, with the « Maphorion » on her head, the small cross on her forehead, repeating on the shoulders, and the ample blue peplum with gilt fringes. A rigid neck supports a thin face with scarcely pronounced lips, very mild but motionless eyes, fixed on the bystanders that, the more you look at them, the more they get life and force, making us forget the reality, space and time in which we live, in a rapid foretasting of the Eternal. Also the Child, holding the roll of the law on his gown, is very pleasant. He is dressed like « basileus » and rests on the Virgin's right arm, from whose hand a white handkerchief, *Mater Dolorosa's*

▶
12 - A detail of the central Apse. The Virgin with the blessing Child (XII-XIIIth cent.)

·MP· Ꙁ ·ΘV·

PORTA SALVTIS PROLE MARIA

symbol hangs: in this way all the elements of the Redemption gather in Mary. On the frame of the arch it still runs the invocation in latin leonine verse *sum Deus atque caro, patris et sum matris imago, non piger ad lapsum set flentis proximus adsum* (I am God and man, the image of Father and Mother, I am not far from the offender, but I am near the penitent).

The mosaic of the Virgin on the apse is perhaps of 1230, the Apostles' mosaics are of 1100, with evident reference to the mosaic techniques of the Church of Aghias Loukas in the greek Phocis. The Annunciation is told on the royal arch plumes, opening the apse. The Angel Gabriele, on the left, is seen in rapid motion, with his arms stretched; on the right the Virgin, long and thin, is caught in the agitation movement and turns pale at the salutation. With her left hand raised and the right one holding the spindle, she stands up from the throne, wrapped in an ample peplum; she lays the shell-drawn work-basket according to the Annunciation usual scheme in Byzantine area, on the ground.

Also this mosaic reveals the same techniques, and perhaps the same hand of the apse, therefore it is of the same period. On the left wall there is an inscription of the first church building, in 639, a precious and rare lagoon epigraphic document; on the right there are some inscriptions of members of the local clergy. Along the corridor leading to the apse of the right side chapel or diaconicon, on the wall, there is a neoclassic small tabernacle for the relics of the Cross and S. Cecilia's head with a shovel of the Cross symbols; the rest is a work of 1500, as the date below proves. The apse of the chapel is full of mosaics. The mosaic is one of the most passionate problems of historical criticism both for the date and the style. Below, it shows the four doctors of the Latin Church blessing i.e. from the right S. Agostino, S. Ambrogio, S. Martino, S. Gregorio Magno, with a small window opened to the East, symbol of the Christ, in the middle.

It is interesting to notice that S. Martino has taken the place of S. Gerolamo perhaps because of the fame and devotion of the French saint in the Middle Ages and the Torcello lagoon after 1000. The first two saints on the right wear brilliant episcopal clothes with ample planets and palliums, while, the two on the left are dressed in pontificals with a crossed golden decoration, a closed book and a maniple in S. Gregorio. They are separated by the tuft of corn poppies in blossom interlaced in different ways.

On high, there is the latin inscription, inspired to some literary texts of the pagan writer Marziano Cappella and to S. Paolino d'Aquileia: Personis triplex Deux est: et Numine simplex, herbidat hic terram, mare fundit, luminat aetheram (God is triple as to persons but one in the Essence. He covers ground with grass, distributes the seas and illuminates the sky).

The mosaic has a didactic function and completes the one of the high apse, where the Apostles represent the Revelation through the Scriptures and the Doctors of the Church through the Tradition, here. They are a very beautiful work, remade at the end of the XIIth cent. on a probable scheme of the IXth cent. The Christ on the throne masters above, in the apse basin, as a lesgilator surrounded by two angels, Michele on the left and Gabriele on the right, like the ones in S. Giusto's in Trieste. The blessing Christ is sitting on an inlaid throne and rests his bare feet on the cloud-worked footstool with the thunderbolt signs. The bearded, stern face follows the byzantine schemes of 1000; it presents the christian version of the pagan theme, i.e. of the Thunderer, the king of Olympus, while here he is the king of the sky and the earth. The whole is of the XIIth and XIIIth cent. but of a different hand from the inferior mosaic.

13 - A detail of the central Apse. The six Apostles of the right side (XII-XIIIth cent.)

14 - A detail of the central Apse. The six Apostles of the left side (XII-XIIIth cent.)
▶
15 - In the following page a sight of the right aisle.

14/15▶

After admiring the geometric embroidery decoration of the apse border look at the important mosaic of the vault. In the four sails of the crossing, four angels support the shield with the mystic lamb. The ones on the left and the right with serene faces stand on a globe (a ball or a world) on the capital of a column; the ones on high and down, with nervous, hieratic faces, are truncated at their calves perhaps owing to the vault rearrangement works made during Orseolo's period.

The *nimbus-girded lamb*, in the blue night sky, with his right hand holds the base of the pastoral cross, hooked under the cross-piece, piercing through his breast, from where the redeeming Blood spouts, while he turns on one side with a vigorous dash. Four flowery bands (symbol of the four rivers of the earthly Paradise) fall from the vegetable plait surrounding him, with lilies, bunches of grapes, wheat grains, alluding to the eucharistic mystery, for which the chapel or diaconicon was used. Within the sails there is a luxuriant floral decoration with ample volutes among which sea-gulls and marshy birds fly and a lynx moves with soft pace; below, on the right and left there are sea-gulls, an eagle, a lion, a bull and a peacock that, if as symbol they allude to the Evangelists, as type they correspond to the identical decoration in the presbyteral vault of S. Vitale's in Ravenna, of the IVth cent. The iconographic motive and the stylistic technique of this mosaic and the one of Ravenna are alike, so the mosaic of Torcello was supposed to be a little later, i.e. contemporary of the first building of the Churches, a work of the workmen of Ravenna. Thus it is perhaps the most ancient mosaic of Venetian lagoons, even if it was restored many a time in the XIIth cent. On the left side of the chapel there is a small tabernacle for the holy oils, with shells and two beautiful dolphins, a part of the primitive building of the VIIth cent. much alike the one in the Eufrasiana of Parenzo. The altar is a fine example of baroque with marble inlaid work; the silver small door is a work of the living Remigio Barbaro from Burano. Then through the small wall door you pass into the annular vault of the central apse, communicating with the left one; now it is impossible to pass because of the stagnant water. There is nothing important in the left apse of the presbytery, except the altar of the XVIIth cent. with the tender stone statues of the Saints: Lorenzo Giustiniani, already on the high altar and S. Antonio from Padua (right) and a pictures of S. Antonio from Padua. On the right of the left aisle there are some graves of canons and in the arch niche, remains of a fresco of the XIIth cent. and of an inscription in honour of the bishop Bono Baldo, died in 1215.

The entrance to the pulpits opens on the left with the typical stairs and the decorative plates of the base. It deserves a particular attention the broken fragment, dealing with the pagan subject of the occasion or *cairos*, running away, while the old, lazy man, smoothing his beard, tries to keep it and a lazy woman grieves for the lost occasion; on the contrary, the bold young man seizes the time and stops it without any indecision. It is of the XIth cent. with roman anticipations and was already a part of the decoration of the most ancient pulpit. Near the door of the sacristy there is a small holy- water basin of the IXth cent.; tre woody altar of Campsa, like the right one, with S. Liberale in the middle, S. Girolamo on the left and S. Antonio from Padua on the right and, below, scenes of the life of S. Liberale and the altar with the shovel of the Virgin, a work of Jacopo Tintoretto. The large mosaic of the wall is worked according to byzantine rules, so that the congregation going out of the church bears the memory of the last destiny according to the warning of the Scriptures: « *remember your last destiny and you will sin no longer.* » (Eccl. 7, 40).

▶
16 - The Right side chapel of the Holy Sacrament. Below there are the four doctors of the Church: S. Gregorio and Martino - S. Agostino and S. Ambrogio; in the central part there are the blessing Saviour on the throne and the Archangels Michele and Gabriele; above: four angels support the Copper Shield with the Mystic Lamb - XIIth cent.

17 - *The Holy Sacrament's Apse: S. Martino blessing; one of the four doctors of the Church.*

18 - *The Holy Sacrament's Apse: S. Ambrogio. A mosaic, on a golden background, for the most part rebuilt on a more ancient plan, in the XIIth cent.*

▶
19 - *Another detail of the mosaic of the Holy Sacrament's Chapel: the blessing Saviour on the throne.*

It is divided into two large parts both for subject reasons and for style ones: the inferior one represents scenes of the last judgment in the first, second, third, fourth fascia and was performed in the second part of the XIIth cent.; the upper one deals with the mystery of Christ's death and his descent to the hell in the fifth and sixth fascia and was performed later, at the beginning of the XIIth cent. For an easier reading follow the proposed division. In the fourth fascia within the almond there is the Christ judge with the Passion wounds; the chest is not bare yet, for this scheme, a German contribution, appears in the following cent; on the sides there are the Virgin and Battista protected by two angels of the Domiration choir, wearing a richly studded with gems clothes.

Two angels of the throne choir support the divine almond and above, the four tetraform beings, remember the four Evangels, according to the scheme of the Syriac miniatures of Rabula. The biblical river of fire, already described by the Syriac poet Commodiano di Gazza, of the IV cent. springs from the almond gurgling and curling in the space to feed the hell below. The twelve Apostles are sitting on a long sofa on the side of Christ, like in the picture of the Vatican picture-gallery, at fixed seats, decorated with fusaroles; they are six on each side, led, on the right, by S. Pietro with the keys and on the left by S. Paolo, holding the book of the epistles.

In the middle of the third fascia it dominates the « Etimasia » or triumph of the cross, placed over the clouds, according to S. Matteo's apocalyptic text, with the symbols of the passion: the lance, the sponge, the crown of thorns and the book of Life put on the altar. Two seraphs keep the cross and two Principati (Angels) the Etimasia, while below the frightened Adam and Eva, symbol of all the tribes of the earth in terror and tears, according to S. Matteo's narration, are worshipping.

On the left and right four angels with blaring trumpets of the kind of the one of the Carolingian Horn, call the death to the resurrection: these, wrapped in their sindons, on the left, come out of the sepulchres and the throats of wild beasts (lions, elephant, hyena, griffons and ravens) like in the Vatican picture.

On the right, the dead of the sea, victims of wrecks rise, in a clear language for a people of sailors and fishermen such as the inhabitants of Torcello.

The womanly figure, emerging from the sea monster with links on her arms and legs, is the symbol of the sea, according to the byzantine scheme. The angel unrolling a roll, is dissipating the starry sky which will fall at the end of times, according to S. Matteo's texts. In the middle of the second fascia S. Michele is weighing the Souls in the classic aspect of the « psicostasia », a theme dear to the East figuration, with the horned demons, trying to make the scale lean to them, throwing the sins from their leather bags; a particular, frequent in the west art from Burgundy to Ireland and Sweden. On the right and the left God rewards or punishes. The legions of the Blessed, in four groups, celebrate Christ for the prize. In the first group on the right there are 14 clergymen among which we can identify: S. Gregorio di Nazianzo and S. Basilio with black beard and hair; in the second group there are 13 martyrs preceded by the richly clothed Saint Teodoro followed by S. Giorgio, S. Demetrio, S. Procopio and perhaps S. Teodoro soldier; in the third group there are eleven monks in Basil clothes, where it is possible to recognize S. Autimio with a bifid very long beard and perhaps S. Antonio priest and S. Saba; in the fourth group there are 14 women, the first is a penitent with long, thin legs and arms (perhaps S. Maria Egiziaca), the second is a nun and the third is perhaps S. Caterina from Alessandria with gems on her head, dressed like the Giovannina of S. Teodoro's train in S. Vitale in Ravenna.

▶
20 - The Apse of the Holy Sacrament's Chapel: four angels support the Copper Shield with the Mystic Lamb. This mosaic, conceived on a Roman-Ravenna composite scheme was renewed in the XII cent.

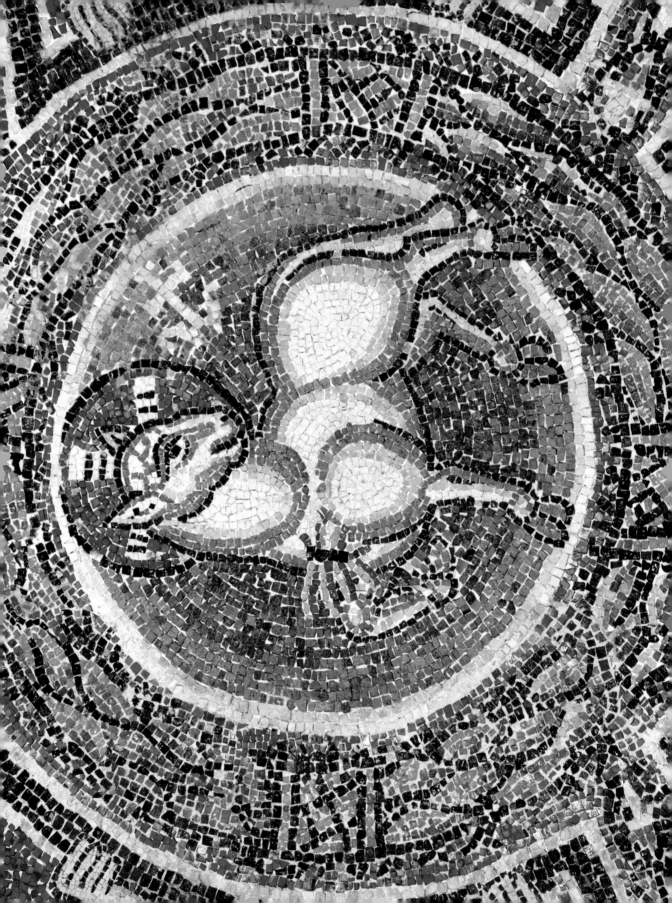

21 - *The Apse of the Holy Sacrament's Chapel: four angels support the Copper Shield with the Mystic Lamb. This mosaic, conceived on a Roman-Ravenna composite scheme was renewed in the XII cent.*

▶
22 - *A decorative detail of the mosaic of the right side Chapel.*

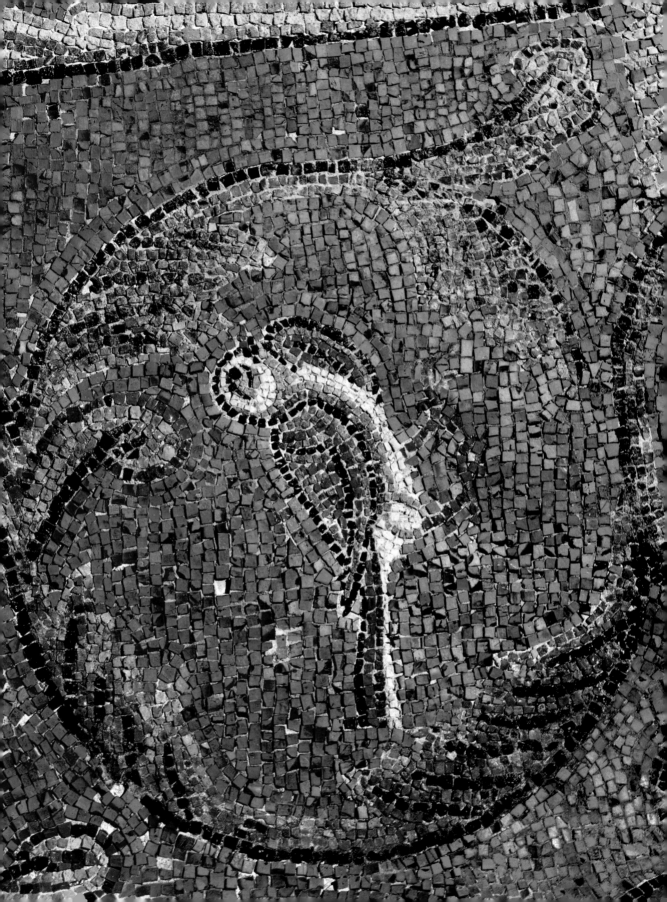

23 - *A detail of the mosaic of the Doomsday: crucified Christ between the Virgin and S. John Evangelist.*

▶
24 - *The large mosaic of the Doomsday in six zones; it occupies the whole bottom facade of the Cathedral. It is a mosaic of Venetian-Byzantine school built in two times, in the XII and XIIIth cent.*

25 - *A detail of the « Doomsday ». The « Deisis » Christ Judge between the Virgin and S. Giovanni Battista, in the glory of the heavenly court.*

▶ 26/27 · *Details of the « Doomsday »; the group of the Apostles near the Christ Judge, behind the angelic groups.*

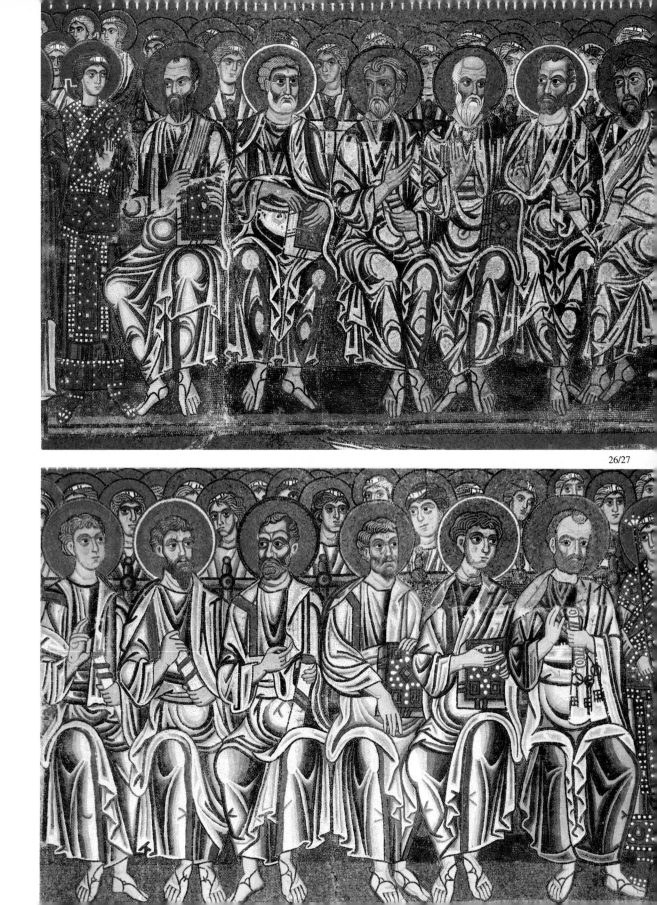

28 - Detail of the « Doomsday ». « L'E-toimasia ». The Divi-ne throne prepared for the Ordeal, worhipped by Adam and Eva and protec-ted by the two Ar-changels Michele and Gabriele.

◀▶
29/30 - Detail of the « Doomsday ». The Resurrection of the Dead. On the left the call to life of the dead from the abysses of the sea, on the right the dead resuscitated from the land.

On the left, two red angels, with impassible faces drive the damned into the fire of the hell by long perches. They are the offenders of pride, punished by seven little devils, allusive to the seven main sins of which pride is the source.

According to a probable interpretation the heresiarchs and politicians are punished here. The emperor, pushed by the angel, is perhaps Costantino I Capronimo (741-775), iconoclast identical in a coeval coin; the bald bishop with a fluent beard is the heretic Nestorio, as he appears in the final judgment at Salamina. On high there is a monk with the beard drawn to the right by a little devil with a despiteful relish, who is perhaps the heretic Eutiche; it follows a head with a slightly grey beard, a casque with mark of gems on top and a headgear, or skiadion hanging by his side; he is perhaps the patriarch of Constantinople Sergio (610-638) an heretic supporter of monothelism, the little devil tries to uncrown. Then there are a diademed queen or basilissa, perhaps the empress Eudossia, who persecuted Crisostomo and that an impertinent devil tries to uncrown and a nun, whose wimple is seized by a devil, gesticulating towards Lucifer. A young man with a west headgear, a prominent chin in the act of making faces, turns to Lucifer.

On his right, another devil seizes an old, bearded man with a coloured or fringed band arab headgear and below a little devil with his hand stretched towards Lucifer in symmetry with the left one, is dragging a men. Lucifer or Ades is sitting in the middle, according to the byzantine scheme. His throne is the back of the biblical monster or Leviathan with very bright blue scales and two heads of he-goat, the devils' symbol as, a century later, the liturgy sings in Dies Irae; it is devouring two women. In his lap on a green flap, symbol of the hope in evil, he carries the Antichrist, as a byzantine basileus, a blasphemous opposition to the Virgin Odegetria of the central apse; Lucifer has his right hand stretched and the Antichrist's replies to his gesture.

Below the throne there are two heads: a man with moustaches, a deformed ear with pendants, plait hair falling from the bare occiput, therefore Mongol and opposite an Egyptian woman, with a polychrome arab turban, and a high blue collar. As we see, it is evident here the principle of deeming damned those who are not baptized, especially the supporters of Islam, echo of the byzantine struggles against them, but in symbolic function of the pagans, at Torcello. Below, in the first fascia the damned suffer, according to the medieval law of retaliation: the lustful among the blazes; an old man, perhaps the rich Epulone, a young man and an old man with a bifid beard (perhaps a Northman); four naked gluttons biting their hands; two wrathful, an old man smoothing his beard and a young haloed man dipped in deep, cold waters; the envious people, reduced to 17 skulls with the imps penetrating into the empty eye-sockets; the misers presented with eleven cut heads; four of them are women's with ear-rings; the decoration of four men's heads with different parting hair and the typical moustaches, still recalls the Mongolian race; then, there are the indolent, ten, considering bones, hands and cut feet. The sense of horrid and macabre predominates in the two scenes of envious and indolent people; it finds a correspondence in the byzantine frescoes of the final judgment in the Apostles' church at Amari, in Creta, a little later than the work of Torcello, as well in the episode of the resurrection of the dead in the Vatican painting already mentioned. As you can see there are the seven main vices in the punishments of Hell, according to the scheme of west theology in relation with the seven little devils already seen; the three main concupiscences, rememberd by S. Giovanni are painted red in the squares: the concupiscence of the flesh (the lustful), the concupiscence of the eyes (the misers), the pride of

▶
31 *Detail of the « Doomsday ». The Angel holding the scales, where men's good and bad actions will be weighed*

32 - Detail of the « Doomsday ». The Virgin praying for God's Mercy.

33 - Detail of the « Doomsday ». The Bishops, the Martyrs, the Monks the holy women, predestinated to the heavenly Beatitude, pray for God's mercifulness.

34 - Detail of the « Doomsday » - The Hell: Lucifer, the Great Proud, seated on a dragon, keeps his son, the Antichrist, on his knees, while the two Angels drive the proud into the fire by their lances.

35 - Detail of the « Doomsday » - The Damned of the Hell; The Lustful: The Gluttons - the Choleric - the Envious People - the Misers - the Indolent

life (the proud). Opposite there is the paradise, the soil of which is covered with corn poppies. S. Peter keeps the keys and S. Michele is represented as « psico-pompo » i.e. leader of souls; near the Paradise door there is a cherub, whose wings are quilted with eyes, while the Good Robber, on the other side, holds the salvation cross.

Then it appears a woman praying, it is perhaps the Virgin. It follows the groups of the elected, portrayed in twelve, according to the text of the Apocalypse (Apoc. 7) among the 12,000 shown to indicate the saved, sent to the Old Man, carrying the Saviour in his lap, opposite as to technique and figure to the Antichrist of the Hell, and then Abraham and his bosom, according to the byzantine schema and the west liturgy motive of the dead. In the lunette, in the middle, there is the Virgin praying or Mother of Mercy with the invocation: *Virgo, divinum natum prece pulsa, terge reatum* (Virgin, pray the divine Child; cleanse from the sins).

Her look is firm and penetrating like the « pendant » of the Mother of God in the apse basin. The second part of the mosaic, i.e. the upper one shows no specific characters on the Crucifixion as it was completely remade by the end of last cent., but the scene of the Descent to the Hell and the Resurrection has a great interest both for iconography and date. The scheme is always byzantine according to the monk Dionigi from Furna's rules at section 306 of this « Treatise on painting » but with some west iconographic annotations. Christ, holding the triumphal cross, has broken the doors of the Hell and tramples upon the devil crouching like a larva under him, very different from the stout one of the mosaic of Daphni in Greece in the XIth cent., while locks and keys are scattered everywhere.

He is holding out his hand to the old Adam, Eva is praying with a coquetry-plaited veil on her head, and a mild face different from the bitter one in Delphi.

On the right Battista, wearing an ample gown points at the resuscitated Christ. Behind him there are the 16 prophets, i.e. the four main (perhaps the first white-bearded is Isaia) and the twelve minor; on the left there are the two haloed kings, David and Salomon, after the Greek rite. Beneath the two groups in two hollows of mount; two young groups, three by three, wearing white tunics, rise their hands to Christ; this particular wants in the scene of Daphni as well in the one to Nea Moni of Chios and is perhaps of west origin, certainly from the Gospel of Nicodemo, but mediated by the apocryphal sermon 160 of Pascha, of S. Agostino and by the west liturgy of the dead, where they insist on the « plausus » of the dead. Also the presence of greek explanations (*E Anastasis*) the only ones in the whole wall, but near the identical proceedings in S. Mark's mosaics, and some stylistic particulars such as the timid presence of the arrow style in Eva's plaits, in Adam, and Christ, his nimbus with gems and his oval face, lead us to date the mosaic in the first part of the XIIth cent. coeval of the apse Virgin. The large mosaic cycle, of venetian technique, even if of remote Syriac origins, presents a byzantine scheme, recalling the scenes of the Giudgment of the damaged small table of Victoria and Albert Museum of London and the ones of the great picture of Vatican picture-gallery, in 1040-1080, and the fresco of S. Angelo in Formis, and other East interpretations like the one of Vorónet in Bucovina of the XIIth cent. West iconographic motives, due to the currents of the Benedictine painting and to subjects of the Gallican liturgy of the dead are included here, in Torcello, on these east schemes. Later the mosaicists ceased every activity in Torcello. Perhaps an economic crisis or the necessity of propping

▶ *36 - Detail of the « Doomsday » - The Paradise - the Patriarch Adam with the souls of the just men - The Virgin praying - The Good Robber - The Door of the Paradise protected by a Cherub - S. Peter with the keys and an angel « Psicopompo »*

▶ *37 - Detail of the « Doomsday » - Christ's descent to the Limbo*

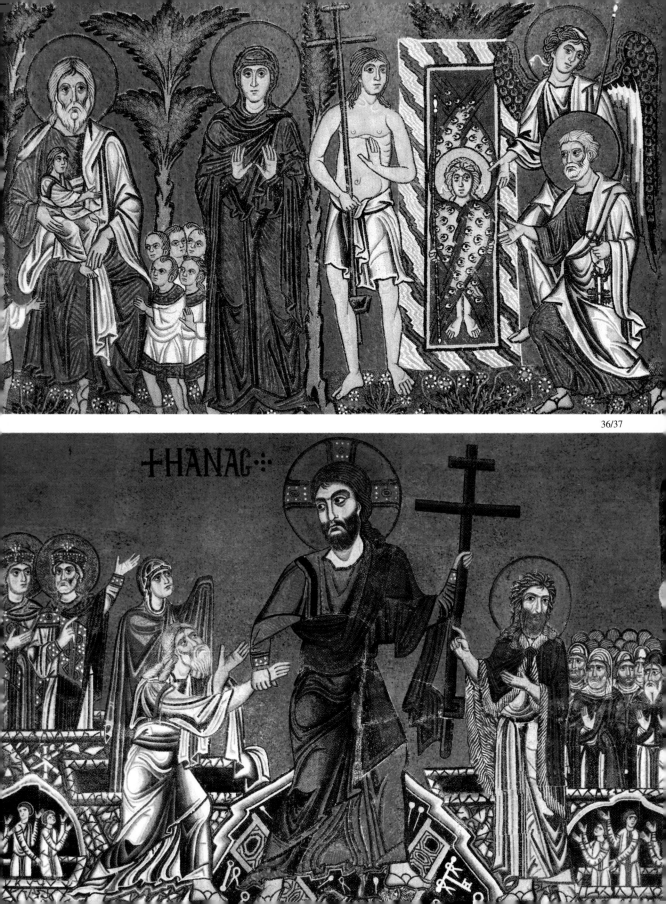

+HANAC∴

38 - Detail of the « Doomsday » - The Victorious Messiah

39/40 Detail of the « Doomsday » - The two Archangels' solemn figures - Above, Archangel Gabriele, on the right Archangel Michele - They hold the labarum with the invocation « ATIOC » (The Holy) in their right hands, and the world in their hands

up the supporting-walls of the central nave of the cathedral suggested to stop the works. On the other side the full decorative development of S. Mark's cathedral in Venice, needed the mosaic workmen. They, probably, went to S. Mark's to continue their « stil nuovo » (new style) inside it.

Near the entrance door there is the stoup (IXth cent.), whose basin is supported by a niello column from where four monstrous animals and four masks hang: the support capital is formed by four human figures, with long tunics, acting as caryatids (XIth-XIIth cent.).

Now the sacristy is used also as Museum of the Cathedral. Among its most important things there are, on the walls, some original pieces of the mosaic of the final judgement, before they were replaced by the present ones in the restoration at the end of the XIXth cent., and the oil series of the twelve Apostles, on canvas, in the inside side of the partition wall, a mediocre work of an anonym of the XVIIth cent. The processional silver cross of the XIIIth cent., and the series of statues, among which the Annunciation (XIIIth cent.) and the Madonna with the Child with a tiara on her head, a rare example of the XIVth cent., of the Virgin considered as Pontifex, have a particular interest. Besides there are the Crucifix of the XVIth cent. and the image of S. Fosca in the peace of death (XVth cent.).

Outside, go on, along the south side of the Cathedral, rising on a big stone base grazing the present parsonage, that is a change of the XVIIth cent. of the ancient episcopate and look at the ten windows of the central nave, open only on this side for light and climate purposes. The harmonious sequence of the apses and back facade opens on the east side.

The ample central apse has got a small apse below, and in the middle a window protected by the defensive lath from waters; from the base four pillars rise; each of the two side apses shows the elegant decoration with four pillars, enlivening the whole surface with a subtle play of motion and colour, repeating the motive of the facade and concluding with a stone small bracket with crosslet.

In the right small aisle the windows are six; the first and the last are without any shutters while the others have a square opening and peculiar shutters, i.e. of Istria stone movable on two big pivots, used, perhaps, in default of panes and for safety. Then you can see the large niche with remains of a fresco of the XIVth cent. All the perimetric wall is divided by big pillars to lighten and decorate the mass of building of barbaric taste. As to the date they saw, in the central apse, probable remains of the VIIth cent., heightened in 1008, while they thought the two side ones of the IXth cent. changed in Orseolo's time, i.e. in 1008 and carried out in different periods, considering the different level of the upper decoration.

In the upper part of the central nave there is a system of blind gallery, formed by five large niches, where the second are double-arched and the central one is very deep. You can see the motive of the facade pillars but here it is resolved in rather plastic values and of a marked roman taste, wheretofore the late decorative whole ranges itself mostly with S. Donato's in Murano. The fourth apse is not in keeping with the rest in fact it was added later, perhaps in full roman period, divided into six pillars.

On its side there is the large quadrangular bell-tower (55 ms. high) of the XIIth cent. near the most ancient lagoón bell-towers in style with the conduit divided into two compartments by a deep « lesenatura » with double small arches and six centring loop-holes in every side but closed on the north one. The cell is formed of three small columns of the same style of the outside ones of S. Fosca with three heraldic bearings on the west side of the XVIth cent. i.e., Torcello; the episcopal heraldic bearings of the Bishop Girolamo de Porcia (1516) and another one with some Keys. Two plait crosses, coeval of the bell-tower are inserted in the upper part of the cell. Above the entrance door there is a roman memorial tablet, inserted in 1008. The inside is characterized by large superposed arches, and by flights of steps you can reach the cell of bells, from where you enjoy the great loneliness of lagoons and sandy grounds, full of sun, green and waters, surrounded by roads and groves. Medieval towers generally testify the power of the town. Here, in Torcello, it gives the same impression of Pomposa and Aquileia, of which it is coeval. Then there is the small chapel consecrated to S. Mark, as, according to the text of the traslatio of the Xth cent., the remains of the Saint stayed here. Its plan repeats a very ancient scheme, i.e. the two side aisles were semicircular and the central one rectangular: the perimetric wall is rectilinear. They are the typical, architectonic forms of the Adriatic zone i.e. the hall-church lacking in apses, going back to the Vth or VIth cent. in Grado and somewhere else and to 1000 and later in Venice and here.

Nay the hint to the small church of the text of S. Mark's traslatio, of the XIth cent., leads us to suppose the building is of this period. Turn to the north and observe the decoration of the sacristy wall and treasure (erected in the XVIth cent.) in the terminal side westward, was interpreted in romanesque « revival » with pillar and upper small arches. So you come back to the grassy central square and can admire S. Fosca.

42 - *The strange lockings of the Istrian-stone pane windows*

◀
41 - *The holy-water basin of the XIth cent. near the central door of the Cathedral*

S. Fosca's

The building, miracolously saved by the destruction decided in 1811 by the French Government, rises on the right of the Cathedral, which it joins by a portico built in the XVIth cent. They thought the baptistery consecrated to S. Giovanni Battista had been built here in 639 and that it was used for the holy rites of the Christian communities running away from Altino. But there are no proofs of this ancient building. Now, the present one is consecrated to S. Fosca, from Ravenna, moved here, before 1011 from the oasis of Sabrata, in Libia, as tradition reports.

We don't know the shape of the more ancient building, acting as martyrium to keep the martyr's remains according to a common scheme in the architectonic complexes of late ancient times and upper Middle Ages.

Bettini states the present building, considering the architectonic profile, is of the XIIth cent.

It presents a very characteristic plan, according to the scheme of the crosswise churches with angle trumptes, like the ones of the byzantine area from Morea to Macedonia: the presbytery and three aisles with apses (the two side ones are the half of the central one) open on the central square room. The two side ones continue in a corridor near the central room; it repeats itself outside acting as polygonal narthex.

From the central flight of stairs you reach the brick, fishbone paved portico, formed of thirteen columns; five of them are polygonal, differently distributed; four are on the entrance side

In former times the columns were joined at their bases by marble plutei, as it appears on the first left side. The cross vault portico insists on the capitals, of different hand and style, which rest on the high structure and recalls similar methods in the Venetian-byzantine arcades of the following centuries in some Venetian palaces (Cà Loredan).

A woody angel of the XVIth cent, rests on the architrave of the central door; on the sides of the door there are two rests of Torcello buildings, one with a small palm, the other with vine-tendrils, works of byzantine taste of the XIIth cent. On the north side there is the high relief with S. Fosca venerated by her brethren, of 1407. Above the portico you can notice the architectonic play harmony of the domes and buttresses. The dome dominates solemn and calm with the hexagonal sail roof and the three centring windows to illuminate the inside and to colour the outside, interrupting the monotony of the whole. The dome rests on four side half-domes insisting on four right angle sectors, driven in four shed facades, with an evident function of push to the mass of building.

All the facades show a white cross with *manus Dei* (God's hand) in the middle of it, to increase the bright, sacred sense of the outside. It lacks the facade for the push on the east side, but in it this function is performed by the complex of the presbytery and the apses, that extends more, considering the plan, because of static purposes. All this system was conceived to build on it a large vault dome, which was never carried out, lest it might fall, as it happened in the similar buildings of greek area, so they decided to build a timber vault with a tile dome. When you enter the stone building, you feel conquered by the gravity and simplicity of the whole, which is the result of a complex play of architectonic elements.

43 - *S. Fosca's Church - A central plan building of the XI-XIIth cent.; surrounded, outside, on five sides, by a porch. It is a unique jewel in Italy like S. Sofia in Costantinopoli.*

▶ 44 - *In the following page there are the « square » of Torcello and the surviving monuments of the island: the Cathedral, S. Fosca's and the ancient Archives*

From the central square room you pass into the round dome, resting on four, large pillars, in the four corners where arcades cross one another. The presbytery (with a large apse) very deep and delimited by two small aisles, continuing in the rest of the building by the marble columns of Cicladi, opens on the east of the central room; on the whole there are twelwe columns with fine corinthian capitals. If they had not used chains as tie-rods, the sense of space would appear more harmonious to show « that great, cultural refinement » Bettini speaks of, in a better way. The only present altar, turned to people, was built in 1970 with marbles of the isle of Marmara, in Ellesponto, in place of the one of the XVIIth cent. put in the Cathedral sacristy in 1915.

On the left side a painting in bad condition represents S. Fosca's martyrdom, a work of the mannerist Giulio del Moro (died in 1610), once on the altar of the XVIIth cent. In the apse you can see the beautiful Virgin with Child perhaps a work of the Ligurian school of the XVIth cent., near the Gagini. On the right there is the tabernacle, to keep the Holy Communion, a work of Remigio Barbaro, still alive.

Along the apse and the upper part of the presbytery, it runs a marble decoration of Cicladi, coeval of the church building.

In the left wall, on high, there is a very ruined painting with the « Assunta » in the middle, S. Fosca ans S. Maura on the right, S. Liberale and S. Eliodoro on the left, a work of a mannerist of the late XVIth cent. On the right wall there is a small votive icon of madonero (XVth cent.) with the Virgin and Child and S. Giacomo di Compostella. On the floor there are three tomb-stones; the one of the podesta of Torcello's daughter (died in 1705); Giovanni Tagliapietra, dean of Torcello's (died in 1753); Gerolamo Cambrotto, local dean's (died in 1696). In the sacristy, added long afterwards the construction of the church and presenting a fine small Sail bell tower, of lagoon style on the south side, that you can reach through a side small door, there are on the wall three remains of transept partition walls, decorated with birds, pecking among the vine-shoots, a fine decorative work, perhaps of the cathedral of the IXth cent. and a fine specimen of woody Crucifix of the XIVth cent. Outside the building, on the north side there is a large niche with three important frescoes of the XIVth cent., with the Crucifixion, three saints, and S. Cristoforo, acting as defence as, those who, going out of the cathedral could observe him, got protection all day long, according to the principles of medieval piety; a sarcopragus with an inscription in honour of Iacomele da Gaggio, cirùco (surgeon) died on March 20th 1426. Outside you can admire the three back apses, forming one of the best examples of the exarch style. The central one is pentagonal, divided into two orders; the inferior is formed by a false portico, got by five arcades, resting on double polygonal columns of the byzantine capital; in the upper one the arches resolve in pillars, on the countrary the central one, acting as a window, is very deep and with a double « risega » (step). The upper part of the central apse has a saw and wolf tooth decoration, of barbaric taste, surrounded by two indented fascias. The raceme central arch has in the middle, within a shield, the blessing *manus Dei* raised on high, a motive repeated in the plait crosses inserted in the facade buttresses. On the contrary on the two minor small apses there is no decoration, with the exception of the ample double-moulded pillar, containing the small, central window.

▶
45 - S. Fosca worshipped by the Brethren of the homonymous school of devotion. A Relief of the XVth cent. walled outside the Church

▶
46 - The inside of S. Fosca's Church (XI-XIIth cent.)

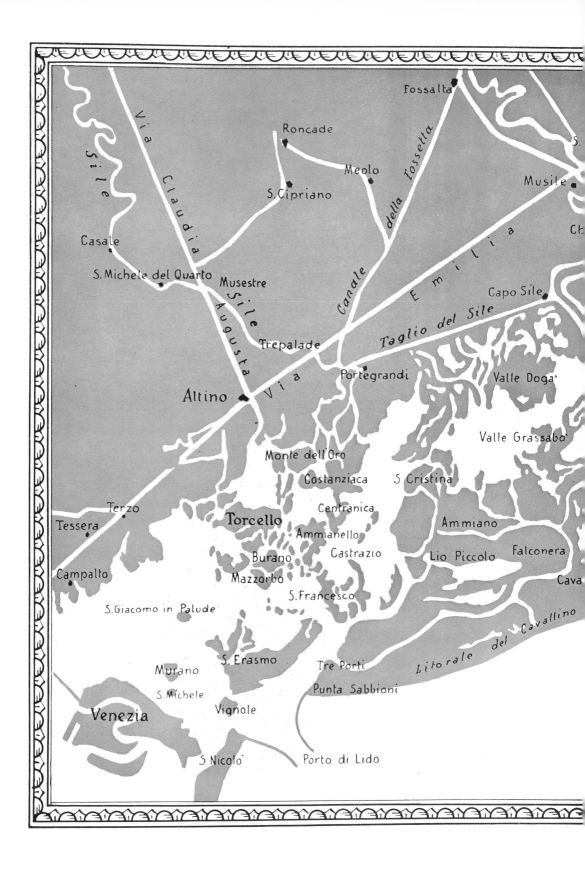

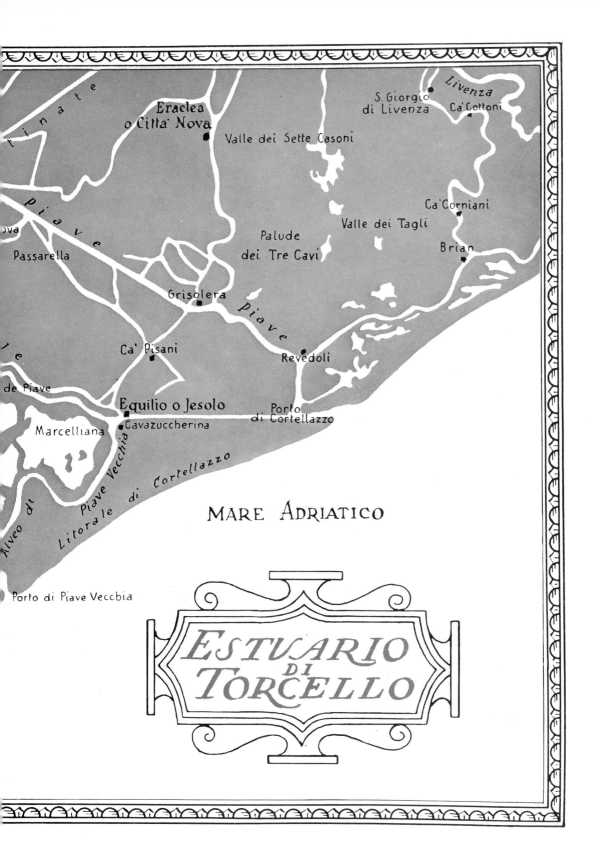

MARE ADRIATICO

ESTVARIO DI TORCELLO

The list of the Deans of Torcello

The diocese of Torcello was suppressed in 1818 and the series of deans, presented here conformably to the data of the Archives of the Patriarch's court of Venice, began

Andrea Minio renounces on February 17th 1822
Pietro Giannelli, June 4th 1822 - died on October 2nd 1828
Luigi Stiore, December 5th 1828 - December 14th 1833
Pietro Simoncin, April 13th 1834 - died on February 18th 1837
Pier Antonio Paulini, April 14th 1837 - December 1st 1845
Francesco Pavan, May 1st 1846 - November 1st 1860
Francesco Bertola, October 23rd 1862 - died on September 30th 1869
Pietro Fratin, April 7th 1865 - December 17th 1868
Giuseppe Meneguzzi, March 22nd 1869 - January 2nd 1873
Tomaso Bertato, April 8th 1873 - February 17th 1876
Francesco Pagamuzzi, April 24th 1876 - August 22nd 1879
Gianfrancesco Zulian, November 18th 1881 - February 9th 1895
Allano Seno, April 8th 1895 - December 22nd 1904
Ettore Manzoni, May 20th 1910 - April 28th 1919
Spiridione Lazzari, June 1st 1920 - 1925
Francesco Tagliapietra, 1925 - 1951
Giovanni Cristofoli, 1952 - 1962
Mario Ferrarese, 1963 – † 1985
Patriarchal Delegation:
1) Don Rosalino Scarpa, 1986

Essential Bibliography

As to the bibliography preceding 1939 you can consult the very good book *of* G. LORENZETTI, *Torcello. La sua storia, i suoi monumenti*, Venezia 1939.
As to problems on architecture and mosaic decoration there is the good book: *Torcello*, Venezia 1940, by M. BBUNETTI, S. BETTINI, F. FORLAŢI, G. FIOCCO.
If you want to get a whole vision of all the problems of the Cathedral and S. Fosca's there is the essay of M. BRUNETTI, Torcello, in « Storia di Venezia », II, *Dalle origini del Ducato alla IV crociata*, Venezia 1958, pp. 597-621. As to the Roman installation problems you can see: L. LECIEJEWICZ, E. TABACZYNSKA, S. TABACZYNSKI, *Ricerche archeologiche nell'area della Cattedrale di Torcello nel 1965*, « Bollettino dell'Istituto di Storia della Società e dello Stato Veneziano », III (1961), pp. 37-47; *Ricerche archeologiche a Torcello nel 1962. Relazione provvisoria*, « Bollettino », cit. V-VI (1963-64) pp. 3-14. On the christian origins: A. PERTUSI, *L'iscrizione torcellana dei tempi di Eraclio*, « Bollettino », cit. IV, (1962) pp. 9-38. As to a too radical interpretation of the apse and diaconicon mosaics; A.M. DAMIGELLA, *Problemi della Cattedrale di Torcello*, I, *I Mosaici dell'abside destra*, « Commentari », XVII (1966), pp. 3-15; II, The Mosaics of the « maggior » apse, « Commentari », XVIII (1967), pp. 273-289; for a general vision: V. LAZAREV, *Storia della pittura bizantina*, Torino 1967, pp. 242, 271. For the mosaic iconologic calls you can consult: G. TOSCANO, *Il pensiero cristiano nell'arte*, Bergamo 1960, I, pp. 323, 360, 370, 394-398, II, 151.

Index of the Illustrations

Before & After
GARDEN
MAKEOVERS

By Vicki Webster and the Editors of Sunset Books

MENLO PARK, CALIFORNIA

Sunset Books

VICE PRESIDENT, GENERAL MANAGER:
 Richard A. Smeby
VICE PRESIDENT, EDITORIAL DIRECTOR: Bob Doyle
PRODUCTION DIRECTOR: Lory Day
OPERATIONS DIRECTOR: Rosann Sutherland
MARKETING MANAGER: Linda Barker
ART DIRECTOR: Vasken Guiragossian
SPECIAL SALES: Brad Moses

Staff for This Book

WRITER: Vicki Webster
DESIGN AND ART DIRECTION: Amy Gonzalez
COPY EDITOR/INDEXER: Barbara J. Braasch
PHOTO EDITOR: Carrie Dodson Davis
ASSISTANT PHOTO EDITOR/PREPRESS
 COORDINATOR: Eligio Hernandez
PHOTO DIRECTOR/STYLIST: Jill Slater
ILLUSTRATOR: Beverley Bozarth Colgan
PRODUCTION SPECIALIST: Linda M. Bouchard
PROOFREADER: Joan Beth Erickson

For additional copies of *Before & After
Garden Makeovers* or any other Sunset
book, call 1-800-526-5111 or visit us at
www.sunset.com

Photography Credits

Cover: Janet Loughrey (see pages 132–135).
Cover design by Vasken Guiragossian.
Page 1: Janet Loughrey (see pages 38–41).
Page 2: Andrew Drake (see pages 98–101).
Page 3: Allan Mandell (see pages 80–83). Page
4, top: Andrew Drake (see pages 98–101);
middle: Frank Gaglione (see pages 128–131);
bottom: Roger Foley (see pages 70–71). Page
5, top: Roger Foley (see pages 52–55); bottom:
Frank Gaglione (see pages 92–95).

Plan for Success

A garden makeover can be as simple as revamping a tired flower bed or as ambitious as tearing out the existing landscaping and starting over from scratch. Whether your plans tend toward one of these extremes or you simply want to add a feature or two, you'll find ideas aplenty in this book. As you study the gardens featured throughout these pages, you'll observe the choices other homeowners have made on what to keep and what to remake in their gardens. Some of these decisions may correspond closely to your own situation. You will also find solutions to landscape problems, large and small. In the process, you'll note the innovative ways home landscapers find to make their garden spaces work for them, whether they want a serene, private retreat, a family playground, or a suitable spot for entertaining—or in a few cases, all of the above.

The styles of the gardens in this book range from cottage casual to sedate and structured. The owners run the gamut from hard-core, hands-on gardeners to novices who could barely tell a petunia from a marigold (before they undertook their recent projects, that is). Some of the homeowners did every bit of the work themselves. Others had professional advice along the way. Still others turned the entire enterprise over to designers and contractors. But all of these before-and-after success stories have one thing in common: Every last project began with good planning.

The Big Picture

Whether you intend to go the do-it-yourself route all the way or get professional help for some or all of your makeover, it will help to begin your planning process with a few basic decisions.

Purpose. How do you want to use your garden? Think about how the space needs to function. For instance, do you want:
• Space for outdoor entertaining?
• Cozy spots for intimate dining or solo relaxing?
• Play space for children or pets?
• Areas for activities like croquet or badminton?
• A swimming pool and/or spa?
• Extensive plantings on which to indulge your love of gardening?

Maintenance. How much time and money do you want to spend on upkeep? Consider plants, hardscape, and outdoor structures in your equation—and, especially if you're new to gardening, figure that both the hours and the dollars will add up to a lot more than you think.

Your taste. Maybe you know exactly how you want your garden to look. If not, take the time to do some homework. Visit friends' and neighbors' gardens, go on garden tours, and peruse photographs in magazines and books like this one. In each case, note which shapes, colors, plants, and materials appeal to you and why. Take photographs, clip articles, and pin sticky notes to pages. The more certain you are of your likes, dislikes, and expectations, the more likely you'll be happy with your new landscape.

Working with a Professional

There is much satisfaction in pointing to a garden makeover and saying, "I did it all myself." The fact is, though, that even if you're an experienced gardener, working with a professional—at least during the design phase—could save you a lot of headaches and considerable time and money. Here are some tips to help you get the most from your relationship with a pro.

Find your comfort range. Consider the complexity of your project, your level of experience, and the size of your budget before deciding how much you want to tackle. You may want to get some basic

design and planting advice from the staff at a local nursery, then grab the ball and run with it. You may go one step further and have them draw up a planting plan. Or you may let a garden designer or landscape architect do the job from start to finish.

Find the right match. When it comes to an undertaking as subjective as your own back (or front) yard, don't settle for the first name that leaps out from the Yellow Pages. Instead, seek referrals from friends and neighbors. Solicit leads from the staffs of upscale nurseries and garden-accessory shops. Or, when a drop-dead gorgeous garden leaps out at you from the pages of a book or magazine, be brazen: pick up the phone and call the designer.

Once you've zeroed in on a few candidates, look at as many examples of their work as you can, in person if possible. Then interview each designer, and choose the one with whom you communicate best. If none of them fills that bill, keep looking; good rapport, especially on a large project, is crucial to achieving results that will make you happy.

Speak up. Even the most talented designer in the world can't read your mind. Give him or her a list that includes the features you want in your new garden, along with your likes and dislikes in terms of specific plant and hardscape materials, as well as general colors, textures, scents, and shapes.

This front **Before** ▶

yard presented a textbook case of the suburban blahs. A two-car garage and asphalt driveway held center stage, backed up by banal foundation shrubs, a utilitarian walkway, and a lawn that stretched, uninterrupted, to the street. The homeowners had a simple, three-part wish list: They wanted character, privacy, and ease of maintenance.

A stately false spiraea (*Sorbaria sorbifolia*) conceals both driveway and garage doors. The shrub resembles a giant astilbe, but unlike that familiar perennial, it thrives in hot sun. At its feet, quaking grass (*Briza media*) casts a silvery sheen. Both plants can spread rampantly, but here the walkway keeps them in check.

The wide walkway of Pennsylvania bluestone over concrete goes head to head with the large-scale plantings. The pavement measures a full 8 feet across.

▼After

Their wishes were granted. Broad, sweeping walkways and beds of low-maintenance plants surround a gently curving—and much smaller—lawn. Tall shrubs ensure seclusion and mask former eyesores.

Hydrangea arborescens 'Annabelle' forms a dense screen between lawn and street. In mid- to late summer, it bears white flowers in clusters up to a foot across.

Reversing the conventional planning order, the designer shaped the lawn first. Then he arranged planting beds and hardscape designed to suit its contours.

▲ Before | When the owner of this house decided it was time to turn her nondescript backyard into a rejuvenating retreat, she called in a garden designer and gave him carte blanche—except for one specific request. She wanted him to fit a swimming pool into the 49- by 69-foot space.

A lap pool gets **After ▶** star billing in a scene that also features a spouting wall fountain, sleek stone terraces, and plantings inspired by the bold foliage and vibrant colors of tropical landscapes.

Garden continues ▶ ▶

Geranium macrorrhizum fills a stone-walled bed. Newly planted, it will spill over the stone wall within the year.

The lower tier includes 'Margarite' sweet potato vine, 'Purple Queen' setcreasea, and 'Bishop of Landaff' dahlias. Behind are 'Black Magic' elephant's ears and yellow coleus.

▲ **The sleek, dark pool** serves a dual purpose in this small garden. Surrounded on three sides by a rich array of vegetation, and adorned with a wall fountain, it could pass for a purely ornamental water feature. But in "real life" it performs daily as a workout venue for a serious swimmer.

▲ **Sedum, angelonia, and catmint** share a poolside bed at the deep end.

▲ **Stone stairs** rise in two stages to a sitting terrace, tucked away behind a thick hedge of heavenly bamboo.

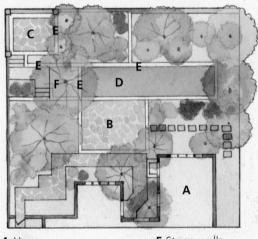

A House
B Lower terrace
C Upper sitting terrace
D Lap pool

E Stone walls
F Raised bed with *Geranium macrorrhizum* and magnolia

▶ **A brilliant wall of vegetation** spills into the water at the pool's shallow end, all but obscuring the flow from a spouting fountain. (An automatic skimmer makes quick work of fallen leaves and petals.)

▲Before

With its white picket fence, manicured lawn, and potted lollypop trees, this garden was a Martha's Vineyard wannabe. And it delivered a resounding slap in the "face" to its actual setting: the magnificent golden hills of coastal California. What's more, the misguided stab at country-cottage charm was completely out of synch with the Arts and Crafts style of the house.

After ▶

Enter a landscape architect who espouses the philosophy that a garden should champion the flavor of its region and the style of the house it adorns. The new scheme reflects the glory of both architecture and ecosystem.

▶ **A built-in sense of order** makes the garden look natural, but not quite wild. An existing locust tree on the left remained, but the designer balanced it on the right with showy, red-spired tower of jewels *(Echium wildpretii)*.

A new front door and fresh paint colors tie the house to its place and its era.

Concrete steps gave way to flagstone stairs, flanked by matching piers. New house colors pick up the stones' tawny shades.

The designer removed the fence, raised the soil level, and constructed a flagstone retaining wall— thereby setting the garden on a sort of pedestal, a maneuver typical of the Arts and Crafts period.

The thirsty lawn gave way to dry-climate natives such as red-hot poker and 'Moonshine' yarrow.

▲ Before

This backyard was everything the homeowner never wanted: a lumpy slope edged with weed-filled beds of scraggly shrubs, and wide open to view from neighboring windows. Against the house, a concrete patio sported an aluminum awning worthy of a down-at-the-heels trailer court. On the plus side, the 30- by 40-foot space was completely enclosed—by the owner's garage and other people's fences, in three different styles.

Dual terraces divide the | After ▶

slope into upper and lower living areas. Reed panels now cover the mismatched fencing, and tall perimeter plantings screen out curious onlookers. The new hideaway even boasts a novel take on the standard hot tub: a vintage claw-foot bathtub that drains into its own dry well.

Garden continues ▶ ▶

The homeowner is delighted with his bathtub. Its scale suits his small space to a T and, unlike a spa, it requires minimal maintenance. Best of all, there is no pump noise or chlorine aroma to sully the scent of flowers and the sounds of trickling water and rustling leaves.

▲ **The gravel-surfaced upper terrace,** in the foreground, houses a dining area, the tub, and a water garden. Just one step down, a lower terrace, paved with flagstone and sheltered by a vine-covered arbor, creates an intimate outdoor sitting room. The stucco house, formerly dull gray in color, was repainted a rich chocolate with burgundy trim to complement the brown tones of the flagstone.

▶ **Space didn't allow for a traditional hot tub,** so the owner opted for a claw-foot, plumbed bathtub. Nestled into a niche in the raised planters, it drains into a dry well made of rubble from the former patio.

16

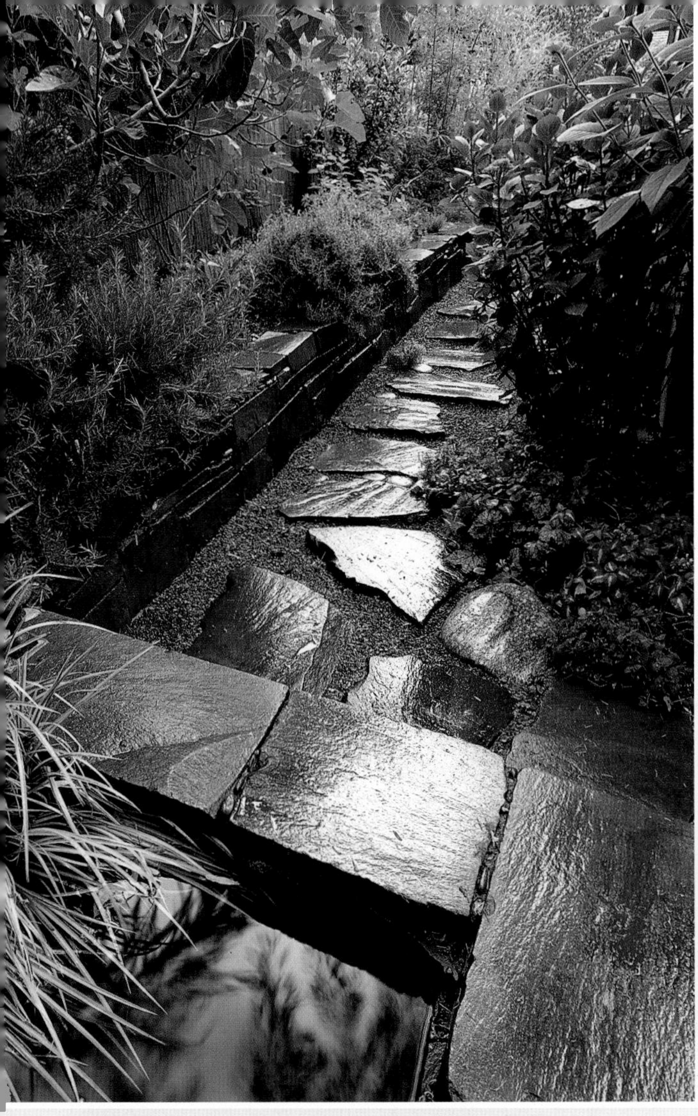

◀ **A stepping-stone path** behind the garage skirts a raised bed made from the same stone that rims the water garden. Dense plantings soften the hard edges and disguise the reed-covered perimeter fencing.

▼ **Low stone walls** that surround the water garden double as extra seating and as space for displaying outdoor art, such as the bronze yogi. Gold-leaved plants shine like beacons against the dark stones and water.

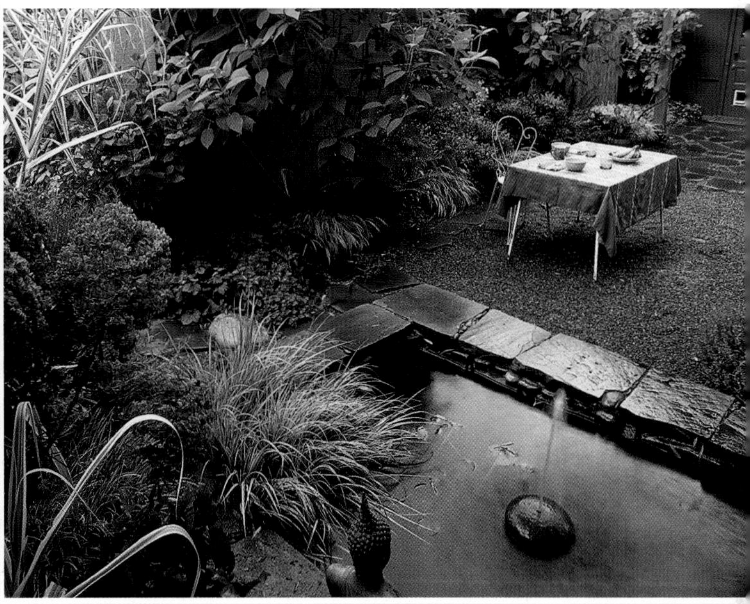

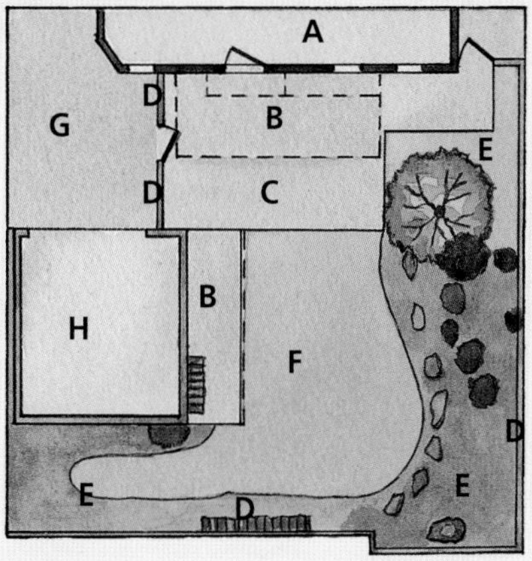

BEFORE

A House
B Aluminum awnings
C Concrete patio
D Mismatched fencing
E Lumpy, sloping lawn
F Areas open to view from above
G Driveway
H Garage

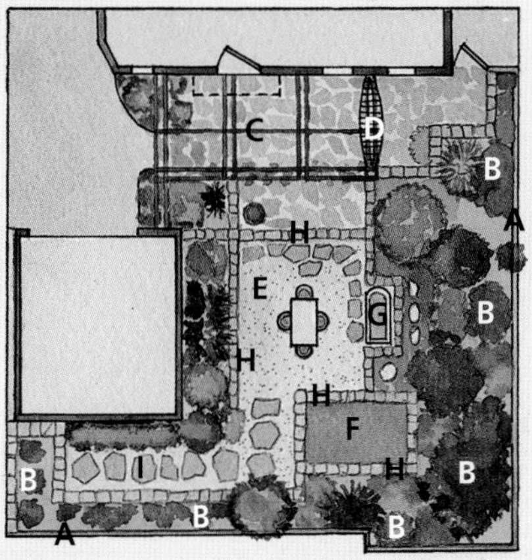

AFTER

A Reed panels over fence
B Tall perimeter plantings
C Lower terrace
D Arbor
E Upper terrace
F Water garden
G Tub
H Low stone walls
I Stepping-stone path

▲ Before

To the new owner of this suburban house, the backyard was a nightmare-come-true. As a psychologist whose days passed in a whirl of stress, she longed to return each night to a haven of quiet and solitude, with plenty of elbow room between her and the nearest neighbors. That wasn't going to happen here—unless she created the refuge she craved.

Wide gravel paths surround the curving beds. The generous breadth makes it easy to maneuver a wheelbarrow through the garden for maintenance chores; the pale color enhances the cool tones of white flowers and variegated foliage.

▲ **Sensory overload** wasn't the only problem this peace-seeking homeowner had to confront. The soil presented an even bigger challenge; much of it was pure mud. Rather than struggle with elaborate (and expensive) drainage improvements, she simply installed a pond in the dampest section.

◄ **A painted sun,** inspired by a quilt pattern, shines its golden light on a clump of ginger lily *(Hedychium).*

The plant list includes, by necessity, plenty of shade lovers, such as elephant's ear, begonias, impatiens, and pentas, along with ferns and hostas.

▲ After | The new space is just what the doctor ordered. Although neighbors remain just beyond the fence, of course, a dense canopy of additional trees blocks visual intrusion, muffles noise, and provides cooling shade. A simple green and white palette and the soft sounds of water soothe frazzled nerves and refresh lagging spirits.

▲ Before

When the owners of this house had young children, the densely wooded lot provided a terrific—and almost work-free—playground. Now, with their brood grown and gone, they decided the time had come for something a little more sophisticated. Topping the list of garden must-haves was more light (which meant a lot of big trees had to go), followed closely by low-maintenance plantings; better parking for guests; and (last but far from least) a spacious, inviting front porch.

With help from a land- ## After ▶

scape architect and a residential designer (who created the porch), the couple got exactly what they wanted: a light-filled, gracious setting where they could relax in comfort, guests would feel right at home—and the work load is almost as light as it was before.

Garden continues ▶ ▶

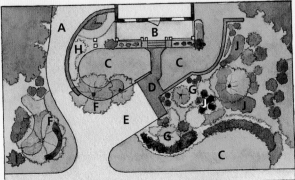

A Driveway

B Front porch

C Lawn

D Brick landing and walk

E Parking court

F Existing oaks

G New crape myrtles

H Azaleas

I Butterfly bush

J Perennials

Basic foundation plantings complement the straightforward architecture of the house and provide evergreen color.

Small patches of fescue lawn provide the first lawn the light-starved site has seen in years.

Topiaries on brick pedestals flank the stairs, visually tying the porch to the garden.

▲ **A new parking court** near the front steps provides ample space for guests' cars. Originally, the owners had envisioned a formal entrance, with a circular driveway directly in front of the house, but their steeply sloping lot dictated an asymmetrical arrangement. (See the garden plan on page 21.)

▲ **A brick terrace,** inset with planting beds, spans the distance from the parking area to the porch stairs.

DESIGN TIP

When a landscape makeover calls for removing trees to make way for structural features, have them taken out, roots and all. If you use the alternative method, felling the trees and grinding out the stumps, you run the risk of leaving large sections of roots that may regenerate— possibly right up through your pavement.

▶ **On the formerly shady hillside,** crape myrtles and a vibrant assortment of perennials bask in the sun. The low-maintenance plant list includes sedum, purple loosestrife, and coreopsis.

▲ Before
When the homeowners bought this property in Washington state, the landscaping consisted of a scruffy lawn, a rotting deck, overgrown English laurels all but crawling through the windows, and huge native trees that kept the whole site dark.

▲ **Yellow corydalis** and purple Siberian iris bloom around a meditating Buddha.

Step one | ## After ▶

in the multiyear transformation entailed taming the laurels and reducing the tree population. Then, with light at last streaming in, came a deck designed for entertaining and a pond stocked with irises, water lilies, and koi. Finishing touches included a small but lush lawn and colorful flowers for both shady and sunny pockets.

In a mostly green landscape, bright banners, blue window trim, and deck-top container plants add welcome jolts of color.

The clear cedar deck can take all the moisture the Washington skies can deliver; its curved lines echo the shape of the pond just inches below.

"Boulders" rimming the pond are made from concrete, sculpted by hand and spattered with latex paint to mimic the color and texture of natural stone. Built-in planting pockets provide homes for water plants.

DESIGN TIP

If you're undecided about major hardscape features, or you're not sure how much time you'll have for plant care, try to plan your garden makeover in stages.

Only some **Before** ▶ minor cosmetic problems held this house back from curbside stardom. First, not a speck of floral color lent sparkle to the pale yellow walls. The spindly wrought iron railing on the porch looked dated, and a downspout visually cut the building in two. Behind an unattractive red-brick wall, a sparse row of foundation shrubs left the gas meter fully exposed, but served no other useful purpose. Finally, with no path leading from the drive-way to the sidewalk, the owners had to traipse across the lawn to reach the front door.

▼ After | From out of the blandness sprang a warm and welcoming cottage. Wooden railings add substance to the porch, and a path, made of bricks salvaged from the wall, curves across the front of the house. Besides making for easier walking, it forms a boundary for a colorful tapestry of annuals and perennials.

Garden continues ▶ ▶

▲ **New wooden railings and a stout column,** stained gray to match the porch, give the entrance a classic look. Old iron fragments (available from architectural salvage and garden shops) add a personal touch.

▲ **Augmenting the foundation planting** with a few new shrubs concealed the gas meter and created a backdrop for colorful annuals and perennials.

▲ **A columnar-form yaupon holly** camouflages the downspout, relocated to the right-hand corner of the house.

▶ **Filled with a mix of flowering plants and colorful foliage,** a wrought iron plant stand brings color right up to the door and softens a blank wall.

28

DESIGN TIP

Bleeding-heart vine, also called glory-bower, is a West African native that thrives in protected sites in warm winter climates. In cooler regions, grow it in a large container and move it to a frost-free shelter for the winter, or adorn your arbor with a hardier specimen, such as clematis, climbing roses, or wisteria.

▶ **In a stroke of recycling genius,** the owners dismantled the angular wall in front of the house and used the bricks to build a gently curving walkway from the driveway to the front door. Leaving some of the mortar intact gave the path an aged look (and also made for less work).

▲ **Two rows of bricks** set on their sides edge the pathway. Leftovers, both whole and broken, make up the paved patches in the center. Crushed, hard-packed stone fills the remaining space, offering a firm surface with good traction, even in wet weather.

◀ **Where path and driveway meet,** an arbor topped with a red birdhouse defines the new garden space and offers a cheery welcome to all comers. Planted at the base of the structure, bleeding-heart vine *(Clerodendrum thomsoniae)* quickly clambered up the posts to deliver evergreen foliage and two-tone, scarlet and white blooms from summer through fall.

▲ Before

If ever a flower bed needed a makeover, it was this one in a sunny suburban garden. The shapeless, 15- by 40-foot plot of heavy soil gave weeds a happy home, but cultivated plants struggled for mere survival.

After ▶

Phase one in the transformation process entailed shaping the space into graceful curves, amending the soil with compost, and installing drip irrigation. Then, with help from a garden designer, the homeowner assembled a roster of triple-threat plants that boast drought tolerance, ease of maintenance, and year-round good looks.

For dramatic color impact without a craz quilt look, the designer advised confining the palette mainly to two flower colors. Vivid pink 'Flower Carpet' roses lead the through the border, while in strategic spc butterfly bush, Mexican sage, and penstemon add bursts of soft purple.

From spring through fall, lamb's ears, artemisia, and society garlic form a silvery backdrop for colorful flowers. In winter (thanks to the garden's mild climate), these evergreens become the border's main attraction.

Single specimens of bougainvillea and deep blue hibiscus soften the board fence and add punch to the sweeps of softer color.

To enliven the border, plants were layered by height, with the shortest growers in front and the tallest ones in the back.

The owners of this house had requests aplenty for their garden designer. Topping the list were summertime quiet and privacy, and no wonder—the property faces a busy, 5-way intersection. The couple also wanted a more level front yard. The existing slope gave them little useful planting space and made mowing a nightmare.

Before ▶

◄ After | Terraces, supported by low stone walls, fill most of the former lawn. Strategically placed trees help muffle noise and filter views from streetside. But passersby are not left out of the picture: Thanks to multilevel planting beds, pedestrians can enjoy the lower tiers while home-owners survey the scene from the porch.

Garden continues ▶ ▶

▲ **For retaining walls,** the designer chose a stone used on many older homes in the area. It gave the new landscape a settled appearance right from the start, even though the house is part of a new development.

▲ **A mainly green and white color scheme** prevails in summer, with bursts of burgundy foliage to carry the eye through the garden. The mounding forms of shrubs and trees echo the curve of the porch.

◀ **Thanks to savvy tree selection,** the garden remains attractive all through the winter. The crape myrtles and river birches look good with or without leaves.

▶ **A young wisteria** begins its climb toward the top of the pergola.

▶ **A new shrub and perennial border** forms a visual barrier between patio and driveway

▶ **Drifts of flowering bulbs** announce the arrival of spring in the Northeast.

When you're shopping for trees or shrubs, read the labels carefully, and choose plants that will be the size you want when they reach maturity, not when you see them in their nursery pots. Also, consider potential spread as well as height. Of course, it is possible to keep a woody plant pruned to the size you want, but that's bad for the plant's health and appearance and time-consuming for you.

◀ **Before:** Although the backyard occupied level ground, it did have a couple of major problems. First, the small space opened onto the driveway, giving incoming cars a full view of the patio, and anyone on it. Second, the developer's construction equipment had compacted the soil so thoroughly that only a complete restructuring would make it fit for any plant's roots.

▼ **A thick stand of white pines,** planted by previous owners, remained in the new scheme because they were stellar guardians of privacy and quiet. Unfortunately, they must be tip-pruned every year to keep their branches from encroaching on the tiny garden. Replacing them with narrower, more upright-growing specimens would mean waiting years for the new plants to mature.

Despite **Before** ▶ its tract-development bland-ness, this Phoenix front yard had two big pluses: cool northern exposure and a stunning view of nearby Stony Mountain. Unfortunately, there was no place to sit and enjoy either. In the owner's words, "It was just a space you walked through in order to get indoors."

First on the makeover agenda was removing a privacy wall that made a boring beeline from the sidewalk to the front door. That made way for phase two: a tinted concrete patio covered with a 9- by 32-foot pergola of stained fir posts and beams.

A small lawn of water-thrifty Bermuda grass snuggles into the niches between berms and sidewalk.

A new sidewalk winds through a series of gentle berms, the highest of which shields the patio. Plants are mostly Southwest natives, including blue yucca, brittlebush, indigo bush, and palo brea *(Cercidium praecox),* with a few non-native perennials like yellow-flowered angelita daisy.

▼After

So he rose to the challenge, converting the standard-issue entryway into a patio, with ample seating and plantings that ensure privacy without blocking the mountain view. Now, the front yard where no one ever lingered has become the household's favorite gathering spot.

▲ Before

Filled with scraggly grass and a single dead fir tree, this backyard looked bleak, all right. In fact, the homeowners admit they used to leave the curtains closed all day long "because it was so gross out there."

After ▶

Bleakness has been banished. Now, flowering shrubs and colorful foliage plants cloak the board fence, lush turf carpets the yard, and stones—ranging in size from pebbles to giant boulders—provide a unifying theme. And the owners are no longer in a state of denial. In fact, they actually plan events around the garden.

Garden continues ▶ ▶

▲ **Multilayered plantings** on the berms add both texture and height to the formerly flat landscape. Stone slabs, cloaked in dwarf periwinkle, step up to a seating area at the base of an oak tree. Behind the concrete bench are pink 'Rosamundi' rhododendrons and white-flowered dogwood.

▲ **Smooth river rocks** form a dry creek bed that tumbles from the fence to the lawn. Along its "banks" are tawny leather leaf sedges, barberries, and white-edged 'Patriot' hostas.

▶ **With one of the garden's** signature boulders in the background, 'Crimson Pygmy' barberry contrasts with 'Goldflame' spiraea.

40

Renovating a garden rarely provides instant gratification. Overhauling a yard this size (86 by 35 feet) would usually take a contractor three to four weeks from planning to installation. Allow another two years for the plants to reach the stage shown in these After photos.

► **Midway between patio and playhouse,** a tall, angular boulder forms a gently bubbling fountain. The water is pumped up from a collecting basin at the base through a pipe hidden in the rock. Soft mounds of astilbe and white-edged hostas add a soft counterpoint to the jagged stone.

▼ **Intended merely to delight** the homeowners' young daughter (which it does), this colorful playhouse also makes a joyful focal point in the landscape.

Sowing Grass Seed

A lawn started from seed won't give you the instant gratification of sod, but sowing is lighter work, and you have a wider range of varieties to choose from.

Gather Your Gear

Determine the best grass for your site, and buy top-quality seed. The package label should indicate the amount you need per 1,000 square feet of lawn; it varies with the type of grass.

Call a rental yard and reserve a sod roller and a rear-tined rotary tiller for pickup early on sowing day. (Whatever you do, don't use a tiller with the tines in front; they're all but impossible to control.)

You'll also need a shovel, garden rake, seed spreader, starter fertilizer, and—if you don't have an in-ground irrigation system—a garden hose with a sprinkler head.

Getting Started

If the soil in your future garden is good loam, you'll want to spread a 1-inch layer of compost over the entire area. For soil that's high in either sand or clay, plan on 2 inches. Because compost is usually sold by the cubic yard, you'll need to do some calculating before you head to the garden center. Here's the basic equation: 3 cubic yards of compost = 1-inch layer per 1,000 square feet. (Always feel free to round up—it's impossible to overdose on compost.)

1 **After spreading the compost** evenly across the surface, till the soil to a depth of at least 8 inches. Then level the ground and rake it to remove large stones and other debris.

2 **Spread the seed** and fertilizer evenly over the soil surface.

3 **Lightly rake** the seed into the soil.

4 **Spread ¼ inch of mulch,** such as compost or straw, over the area, and then press the seed into the soil using an empty roller. (Don't use sawdust or peat moss; when they're wet, they tend to form a crust that is difficult for seedlings to penetrate.)

For the first two to three weeks after sowing, keep the top ¼ to ½ inch of soil moist, but not wet. If your schedule (or sprinkler system) permits, mist the seedbed lightly from three to five times a day. Otherwise, water at least twice, in the morning and again in late afternoon.

▲ Before
At one time, this backyard must have been a pleasant retreat, but when the current owners arrived on the scene, they found a sorry sight, to say the least. The inventory included a decrepit pool with crumbling concrete decking, an ugly chainlink fence, and a big patch of mucky soil.

The owners | After ▶
called in a garden designer who transformed the near-ruin into a hideaway worthy of a four-star resort, complete with broad terraces, revamped pool, bubbling fountains, and luxuriant plantings.

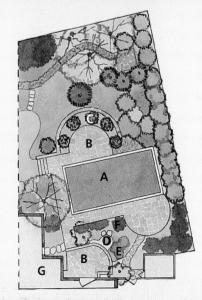

A minihedge of *Pieris japonica* sits on slightly higher, drier ground.

A bog garden proved a simple solution to the soggy-soil problem. A gently bubbling fountain shares the spotlight with a carpet of creeping Jenny.

A Swimming pool
B Terrace
C Rose garden
D Fountain
E Bog garden
F *Pieris japonica*
G House

The aging pool got a stem-to-stern makeover, with new coping, interior tile, plumbing, and support equipment.

The roses, all hardy, low-care varieties, include 'Carefree Wonder', 'Fairy', and 'Scarlet Meidiland'.

Pots around the table hold red million bells (*Calibrachoa*).

A flagstone terrace, enclosed on three sides by a rose garden, replaced the old concrete decking.

▲Before | One step

down from the kitchen door, and wide open to the street sat a sloping, 18- by 70-foot strip of dirt. French doors from the living room led to a balcony that looked down on the sorry sight. Instead of what they called a "no-man's-land," the owners wanted privacy, an area for outdoor entertaining, and access from their living room.

They got it. | ## After ▶

A 6-foot-high wall turned the public space into a private courtyard. A two-tiered patio, with entrances at both kitchen and living-room levels, forms cozy—but far from cramped—seating and dining areas. A savvy selection of big, bold plants softens the walls, avoiding what could have been a jail-like feeling in this narrow space.

Garden continues ▶ ▶

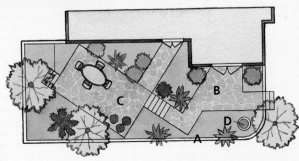

A Wall

B Upper patio

C Lower dining patio

D Fountain

▲ **The bold architecture** and colors of the house dictated the garden's tropical style and vibrant color palette. The star attractions here include 'Tropicanna' canna, lime green flax, New Guinea impatiens, orange flowering maple, and red dahlias.

▶ **A stairway connects** upper and lower patios. Flagstone paving visually unifies the space, but the two levels function as separate rooms, thanks to the sloping, densely planted beds between them.

▲ **Specimen plants** like this statuesque banana, seen against the white stucco walls of the house, function almost as works of art.

▶ **The plants would be seen close-up** so each one
needed to shine. That meant using plenty of dramatic
foliage and intense color, primarily in vibrant shades
of red, orange, and yellow.

▼ **The lower terrace,** just outside the kitchen, sits at
a 45-degree angle to the house; as a result, the space
seems bigger than it really is.

Briza media blooms in May and June; then it's mowed to the ground before the flowers can set seed. That's crucial because, in the designer's words, this grass "reseeds to the point of pain." The foliage grows back quickly, making a stunning backdrop for later bloomers.

▲ Before

When the current owners found the place, the lawn was struggling for survival, trees hovered near death, and flowers were non-existent. Furthermore, deer were dining on everything they could reach.

After ▶

Rather than install a fence, which the owners didn't want, the designer addressed the deer problem by filling spacious new beds with plants that hooved herbivores rarely bother with. Then he replanted the lawn and installed a curving walkway to a relocated entry.

A Chinese elm (*Ulmus parvifolia* 'King's Ransom') in a round bed echoes the walkway's curves. Colorful, shade-loving annuals change from year to year.

The classic combination of white flowers and silvery foliage sets a welcome cool tone in midsummer. Here, the deer-defying stars are garlic chives, angel's trumpet, and rosemary.

An 8-foot-wide walkway, made of brick edged with flagstone, provides a gracious welcome and serves as a focal point in the landscape.

◄ Before
When the future owners saw this house, it was love at first sight—until they looked out the back door and realized that people in four other houses had a bird's-eye view of the backyard. Not that it was much to look at, with its weed-choked lawn, ill-conceived deck, and skimpy brick patio. The couple walked away and continued searching. And searching… In fact, they toured more than 40 places before deciding to "buy the house we love and get a great landscape designer."

◄ After
Now they love the garden even more than the house. But then, who wouldn't love a secluded retreat complete with a gracious veranda, intimate dining terrace, exuberant flower garden, and four-hole putting green?

Garden continues ▶ ▶

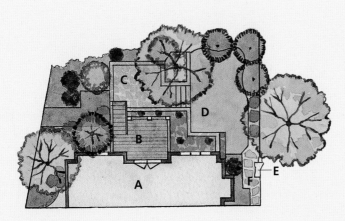

A House
B Veranda
C Dining terrace
D Putting green
E Gate
F Stone path

The dining terrace gains seclusion from densely planted evergreen trees and an ever-increasing array of shrubs, perennials, and annuals.

▶ **A path of Pennsylvania bluestone** (the same pavers used on the terrace) leads from the putting green to the front of the house. *Mazus reptans* fills the gaps between the stones. The Himalayan native thrives on heavy foot traffic and remains evergreen in warm climates.

▼ **A putting green,** made of artificial turf, sits just three steps below the terrace. Besides giving the owners a chance to practice their putts and chip shots, the green has a few other advantages over the lawn it replaced: It never needs mowing, weeding, or watering.

DESIGN TIP

Any small yard with a very slight slope has the potential to house an artificial putting green. But the complex installation procedure is not a do-it-yourself project. To find a contractor who can do the job for you, search the Internet or look in the yellow pages under "Golf Course Architects."

◄ Before | This place falls into the blessing-in-disguise category. How so? Well, when a yard is bland, a little overgrown, or simply not quite *you*, it's easy to drift along without the re-do that would make it your dream garden. On the other hand, when a space looks more like a war zone than a backyard in a good neighborhood, procrastination is not an option.

Jasmine and trumpet vines cloak the fence. Joining them in the raised bed are asparagus ferns, azaleas, and lavender.

A wooden arbor, left from the original garden, shades the kitchen and dining area.

Wisteria climbs up the post toward the top of the arbor.

Brick-capped stone walls double as seating until the furniture arrives.

▼After | From out of the ruin sprang a sleek outdoor living space, complete with a fully equipped kitchen, tiny lawn, and pocket-size pond.

▶ **A raised bed,** constructed of large rocks, holds a young maple tree, New Guinea impatiens, geraniums, white bacopa, and an asparagus fern.

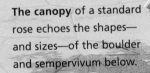

The canopy of a standard rose echoes the shapes—and sizes—of the boulder and sempervivum below.

▲ **Just steps from the party room,** a stone-slab bench nestles into its own secluded niche, backed by a fence swathed in Lady Banks roses.

◀ **A yellow echeveria** marks the edge of the little pond, with rushes rising from the center.

When the current  **Before** ▶

owner moved in, this yard was
"a tangle of oaks and maples" that
left little space—or light—for the

planting beds
she craved.

What's more,
the hardscape
had deteriorated
to the point
of danger, and
the house's
mustard-colored
paint was flak-

ing off (hardly a suitable backdrop
for a lush garden). A narrow, and
slippery, brick walkway extended
across the front of the house to
unattractive concrete stairs and
a small stoop. Hostas and pachy-
sandra thrived in the low light,
but other plants had to struggle for
survival.

Garden continues ▶ ▶

▼ **After** | Item one on the makeover agenda: stripping off the old paint and replacing it with a gray stain. Then, the owner removed some trees and replaced the brick path with one made of stone—thereby making room for wider beds filled with colorful, sun-loving plants.

◄ **Before:** Stone retaining walls, built by the home's former owners, were starting to crumble. The stairs leading from the drive-way to the brick path hovered on the brink of collapse.

▶ **A new walkway** of quarried-stone slabs sits farther out from the house than the old brick path, leaving plenty of room for plants.

▼ **Quarried stone slabs,** like those used at the house entrance, rise gradually to the new flagstone walkway.

◄ **Boulders,** gathered by the owner, form a rock garden with a multitude of plant-ing pockets for spring bulbs and ground-hugging perennials. Plants includes sedge, ferns, carpet bugle, lamium, coral bells, tulips, and grape hyacinths.

▲ **Gazing balls,** scattered throughout the garden, reflect the ever-changing patterns of sky and landscape.

▲ **To give the garden year-round interest,** the owner relies on a varied roster of evergreen shrubs and a changing array of container plants.

▲ **The walk widens out** into a patio just big enough to hold a table for two.

Laying a Flagstone Path

Unless the style of your home and garden is extremely formal, classical, or symmetrical, a curvaceous flagstone-and-gravel walkway can be the perfect path to your front door.

Gather Your Gear

Measure your proposed walkway, and purchase enough sand, flagstone, and landscape fabric to cover the area. You'll also need gravel, ³⁄₈- by 6-inch redwood benderboard, and wooden stakes roughly 10 inches long.

Getting Started

Start by outlining the path with powdered limestone, gypsum, or white flour. Lay out the stones and shift them around until you achieve a design that you like and that requires the least amount of cutting. Remove the stones and set them to the side, maintaining the pattern. Then cut the stones as necessary.

Excavate the soil to a depth of 4 inches, and tamp or roll the surface to firm it. To install benderboard, drive stakes the desired height of the edging at 2- to 4-foot intervals along the pathway and then screw the board to them. (If necessary, soak the benderboard in water to make it more flexible.)

1 **Roll out landscape fabric** on the path to suppress weeds, and tuck the edges firmly under the benderboard.

2 **Pour a 2-inch-thick layer of sand** over the fabric, and rake it smooth. If the soil in your area freezes, lay down 4 inches of gravel first.

3 **As you rake**, moisten the sand with a fine spray of water. Take care not to disturb or saturate the sand.

4 **Tamp or roll the moist sand**, making several passes to pack it down well.

5 **Arrange the flagstones** on the sand, and wiggle them in until they are firmly embedded. As you go, check to ensure that they're level.

6 **Fill the spaces** between the stones with gravel. To help hold the stones in place, use something small, such as decomposed granite.

▲ Before | This barren
little plot was the least attractive
yard on the block. It also held a
lawsuit waiting to happen, with
a dangerous drop-off between the
front walk and a deeply recessed
driveway.

The homeowner designed and built the fence, stepping the 3-foot-high segments to accommodate the sloping street. (A single, 4-foot-high section encloses the porch.)

Spanish lavender, planted along the sidewalk, softens the fence and adds a unifying element to the boisterous cottage garden within. Fragrant, deep purple flower spikes appear in spring and early summer over gray-green foliage.

◄ A curving flagstone path, dotted with Corsican mint, leads to the front door. On the way, it threads through a cottage garden filled with low-maintenance winners such as New Zealand flax, sedge, sunrose, thyme, and 'Amy' and 'Autumn Glory' hebe.

Two more fence softeners stand on the left side of the garden: Gold-and-green-leaved variegated potato vine bears white flowers throughout the growing season. *Senecio greyi* offers gray-green foliage and a profusion of yellow summer daisies.

▲ After | Like the Ugly Duckling, the place has been transformed.
The neighborhood eyesore has become one of its most charming entry gardens.
All it took was some clever plant selection, a new flagstone entry path, and
a homemade lattice fence that runs along the sidewalk and driveway.

▲ Before | When a

Connecticut couple bought this
1920s house in northern California,
they gave little thought to the
standard-issue lawn that came with
it. Why would they? It was just
like the one they'd had back home.
Furthermore, everybody else in their
new neighborhood had a similar
patch of green. So for years, they
mowed, fed, weeded, and watered—
and watered…Finally, tired of having
their lives revolve around their grass,
they ripped it out and replaced it with gravel and drought-tolerant ground covers. That solved the maintenance issue, alright.
But one problem remained: The new scene still packed all the
visual punch of vanilla ice cream.

▲After | Now passersby stop to gasp, often leaving "I love it!" notes in the mailbox. The transformation began when the wife, a metal sculptor, painted the house in brilliant hues to showcase her outdoor art. The result so impressed a family friend, who happened to be a garden designer, that he volunteered a makeover for the yard.

Garden continues ▶ ▶

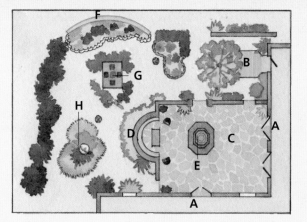

A House
B Sculpture studio
C Inner courtyard
D Curved bench
E Fountain
F New stucco wall
G Dining area
H Angel

▲ **A collection of succulents** thrives in a planter made from an old lawn chair, embellished with trowels and hand rakes.

◄ **In her previous "life,"** this angel was a water heater. Now she stands watch over an island bed filled with New Zealand flax and ornamental grasses.

▼ **Terra-cotta roof tiles,** left over from an earlier repair job, edge a raised bed of *Senecio greyi*. The house marker and patchwork sphere, like all the owner's creations, are fashioned from scrap metal.

▲ **A curved stucco bench** forms one wall of the inner courtyard. Painted in the same jewel tones as the house, it glows in light filtering through the oaks and other large trees behind it.

▶ **A venerable fountain,** original to the house, stands in sharp contrast to its terra-cotta base. The bright red sphere nestled among the foliage is a bowling ball the owner painted red.

DESIGN TIP

This garden owes its success to a masterful use of color. Casting convention to the wind, the house wears vibrant tones usually confined to flowers and accessories. Plants and the owner's artwork steady the picture with their lower-key shades of gray, bronze, and brown.

The owners **Before** ▶ ignored this desolate yard for years because they weren't sure how long they'd be keeping the small, unremarkable house that went with it. A decision to stay for the long haul threw the outdoor flaws into sharp focus. That scruffy wasteland had to go—and fast.

As if by magic, **After** ▶ the garden makeover changed everything. Not only did it turn an eyesore into a miniparadise, but it also gave the owners a whole new outlook on their home. In the words of one of them, "It's still the same plain, unattractive, boring building, but somehow the garden has made it fabulous."

Flagstones in a "crazy" pattern are the perfect choice for a site with odd angles·and quirky spaces. They're also easier to work with and less costly than neatly trimmed squares and rectangles.

An octagonal pool holds water lilies and a thriving family of koi. The L-shaped extension (partially hidden by the shrubbery, but clearly visible from the owner's office window) contains a bubbling fountain and more aquatic plants.

The original board fence remained in the new scheme, enclosing the 30- by 70-foot space. Tall trees just beyond it keep the site in shade for much of the year.

Shade-loving shrubs and perennials fill the beds that rim the terrace. The large pot holds a 'Gartenmeister' fuchsia—the only variety the owner has found that performs reliably in a hot, humid climate.

Red double impatiens bloom nonstop in the low light.

▲Before | The couple who

bought this property loved the house and the neighborhood. They even saw big potential in the ill-conceived backyard, with its domineering driveway. They knew that with a little imagination they could turn the space into an intimate garden where they could relax and entertain their friends, and their two small children could play.

The new garden | ## After ▶

has it all. A new stairway, just outside the kitchen, leads to a dining terrace surrounded by a curving lawn and beds of fragrant flowers. A jasmine-draped arbor divides the driveway from a lower level that holds more planting beds and a barbecue. *Garden continues ▶ ▶*

▼ **A stone birdbath** provides a focal point in a bed filled with vines, evergreen shrubs, and a few bright flowers. Honeysuckle climbs the fence, with pittosporum and Mexican sage below. Annuals in the foreground include bacopa, gerbera, and African daisies.

▶ **On the upper terrace,** gentle curves set a relaxing tone, replacing the yard's straight lines and sharp angles. The shape repeats in the dining patio, small lawn, and even in the rounded rocks that form the raised beds.

◀ **New Zealand flax,** rockrose, African daisies, and photinia line a bed at the top of the stairs.

DESIGN TIP

When you acquire a house with an unattractive—or downright dysfunctional—yard, it's tempting to opt for a quick fix. Resist that urge. Instead, do what the owners of this garden did: take the time to decide how you really want to use your space, not merely how you want it to look. Chances are you'll avoid a lot of frustration down the road (and save money, too).

◄ Before | Only

a tiny patch of grass separated this house from the street. The owners had always felt a little too open to passing traffic, but when a hurled rock came crashing through their front-facing bedroom window, they knew something had to be done.

That "something" took the form | After ►

of multilevel planters and a walled patio that doubles as a sheltered front entry. Besides enhancing the appearance of both house and street, the new design eliminates the need for mowing the lawn—a chore the owners were delighted to remove from their weekly to-do list.

◄ **Behind the higher wall** is an outdoor living room complete with fireplace and wicker easy chairs. A white iron railing provides an edited glimpse of the street—just enough to maintain a sense of both seclusion from, and connection to, the neighborhood.

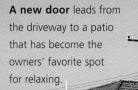

A new door leads from the driveway to a patio that has become the owners' favorite spot for relaxing.

▲ **Stairstepping planters** flank the driveway, adding welcoming color and texture to the smooth stucco walls.

Building a Raised Bed

Besides adding architectural interest to your garden, raised beds allow you to amend the soil to improve drainage, alter pH, or add nutrients far more efficiently than you can in open ground—thereby increasing your planting options immeasurably.

Gather Your Gear

Measure the space your raised bed will cover, making sure that you can reach into the bed's center from either side, and buy your lumber. You will need two 2- by 6-inch boards for each side, 4 by 4s for end- and mid-posts. You will also need ½-inch steel stakes, rustproof nails or screws, an electric drill, a hammer or screwdriver, sledgehammer, hacksaw, wood saw, carpenter's level, and shovel.

Getting Started

Dig shallow trenches around the perimeter of the area the bed will occupy. Its sides should extend about two inches below the soil level.

To the extent that you can, loosen up the soil in the site. This way, you'll be able to mix the existing soil with whatever you use to fill the structure, creating some transition between new and native soils, and making it easier for roots to penetrate deeply.

1 **Cut 2 by 6 lumber** and 4 by 4 end- and mid-posts to length. Use an electric drill to make pilot holes for nails or screws.

2 **After attaching boards for one end** to the posts, set that section upright. Then nail or screw on boards for the sides of the bed to the support posts, being sure the side boards cover the butt ends of the end boards. Finish with the other end.

3 **When the bed is fully assembled**, set it onto the site, pushing the sides into the trenches.

4 **Adjust the bed's position**, making sure the top is level, and using a shovel to move soil as necessary.

5 **After the bed is in place and leveled**, use a sledgehammer to drive a ½-inch steel stake up against each side and end to anchor the structure in place.

6 **For a finished appearance**, cap the bed with 2- by 6-inch finished lumber. Mite the corners; then use an electric drill to make pilot holes for screws or nails.

Before | The couple who bought this riverside property wanted a large, comfortable area for outdoor entertaining. But that presented a slight problem: By state mandate, they could do no work in the river's hundred-year flood plain, and that left them with a strip of ground stretching just 30 feet from the house to no-man's-land. They called in a garden designer, explained their dilemma, presented their wish list of features—and hoped for the best.

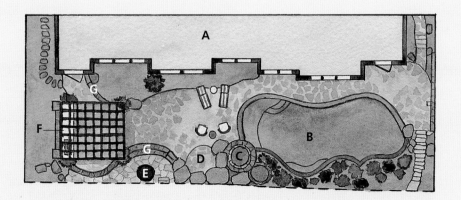

A House
B Pool
C Spa
D Water garden
E Fire pit
F Kitchen, with arbor above
G Stone seat wall

▲ **After** | In a masterful use of space, the designer worked in every item on the list, including a vanishing-edge swimming pool that extends exactly to the 30-foot boundary line. There's a water garden, a spa, and even a complete outdoor kitchen, tucked under the pergola.

Garden continues ▶ ▶

▲ **Intimate seating areas** ensure family-style comfort, but the lightweight furniture can be whisked away to provide more floor space for large gatherings.

▶ **Before:** Tapping into the side yards to gain living space was out of the question for one simple reason: they were almost nonexistent. The house reached almost to the property lines on both sides.

▲ **The boulder-rimmed pond** holds hardy water lilies.

▶ **A basket of colorful annuals** hangs from each of the pergola's support posts. In-ground plants include cannas, coleus, cosmos, and twinspur.

This dismal little **Before** ▶ house rated a big thumbs-down from streams of would-be owners. But the couple who finally bought it saw beyond the scruffy yard and unwelcoming entry. They knew they'd found a gem: a cottage in a good neighborhood, that needed only a minor facelift to put it on a par with its more handsome—and costly—neighbors.

Now the place all but **After** ▶ shouts "curb appeal!" With a new color scheme as their springboard, the owners built a new landing and a simple trellis, replaced the old awning, and painted the front door. Then they added curving beds that surround the entry like a welcoming hug.

▶ **Dark mounds of heavenly bamboo** form a backdrop for the lighter tones of southern shield fern, 'Helleri' holly, and 'Powis Castle' artemisia. Black-eyed Susans surround the landing, with Queen Anne's lace and Joe Pye weed against the house.

Containers of bright annuals change with the seasons. Here, pots of marigolds and 'Gold Mound' lantana line the steps.

A low landing, 7-feet long by 4-feet wide, replaced a broken bottom step. What appear to be marble slabs are concrete pads with every other square stained black. Finally, removing the wrought iron railings, which hemmed in the small stoop, gives the whole scene an open, inviting feeling.

A Natchez crape myrtle repeats the doorway's strong vertical line and, along with the trellis to the right of the door, helps balance the lopsided architecture.

A new, higher, bubble awning shows off the door, freshly painted a deep copper and decked out with gleaming brass hardware. Can lights, set into the shallow overhang, shine directly down on the entryway.

▲ Before | A dark tile roof

and floor-to-ceiling windows with wooden shutters said "Spanish colonial," but the white wrought-iron railing looked more in keeping with a roadside motel. Two monstrous arborvitae trees all but blocked the front door, and behind the low wall, an overgrown boxwood hedge consumed much of the courtyard.

The owners ended | # After ▶

architectural confusion by replacing the iron with wooden beams and railings. Next, they removed the arborvitaes and ripped up the lawn, setting the stage for a revived courtyard and a flourishing Mediterranean-style garden in the front yard.

Garden continues ▶ ▶

▲ **A new walkway meanders** through a striking mix of plants chosen for year-round variety of color, texture, form, and fragrance. Key players include dymondia, yellow angel's trumpet, bronze New Zealand flax, evergreen dogwood, desert spoon, and *Mahonia lomariifolia*.

▲ **Sacrificing the arborvitaes** opened up the entrance, but the two-story house still needed large trees to anchor it to its surroundings. To solve that problem, the owners splurged on five tall palms, which gave the new garden instant drama.

▶ **Strategically placed boulders** add substance to the composition; their soft gray tones provide a perfect foil for the multitude of foliage colors.

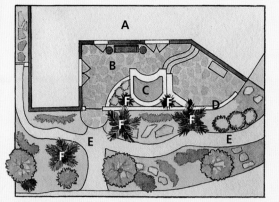

A House
B Courtyard
C Fountain
D Existing wall
E New walkway
F Palm trees

▼ **Inside the courtyard,** the rampant boxwood and a patchy lawn gave way to a multilevel flagstone patio and curving fountain. Its wide walls serve as extra seating.

Before
This yard, behind a 1926 Craftsman house, boasted sturdy masonry walls and handsome, mature plants that screened out unwelcome views. Unfortunately, that ideal perimeter enclosed a tired, aging lawn and broad swathes of broken-concrete pavers.

After
The owners ripped out the pavers, dug up the turf, and sectioned the ho-hum space into several inviting areas— among them, this idyllic dining nook.

Pittosporum shrubs, retained from the original planting scheme, cloak the wall and filter out neighboring houses.

Limestone tile, set in sand, made for an all-but-instant floor.

Lavender, rosemary, and other Mediterranean herbs whet diners' appetites with their delicious aroma—while pleasing the homeowners with their water-thrifty ways.

DESIGN TIP

If your "before" garden lacks healthy, mature trees or shrubs, consider investing in a few, even if it means cutting corners elsewhere. They don't come cheap, but nothing else can impart quite the same feeling of grace and permanence.

Billowing mounds of red fountain grass add a soft, sensual touch, especially when a breeze sets them swaying gently.

▲ Before | This rambling

ranch house, built in the early fifties, came equipped with the era's quintessential front yard: a patch of grass, a bland concrete walkway, and masses of clipped evergreen shrubs. In back, the land sloped steeply downhill, shaded by huge, ancient oak trees. The owners wanted an open, light-filled—and lighthearted—space where they could entertain and the wife could indulge her passion for gardening.

▶ After | With help from a

designer who advises all her clients to "think outside the box," the couple turned the front yard into a haven for plants, people, and an ever-growing collection of whimsical garden accents. Garden continues ▶ ▶

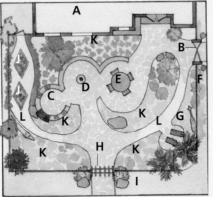

A House

B Driveway arch

C Barbecue patio

D Fountain patio

E Dining patio

F Driveway

G Seating terrace with giraffe

H Entrance arch

I Street

J Raised vegetable beds

K Annuals, perennials, and shrubs

L Decomposed granite path

▲ **The six-foot iron fence** keeps deer out, lets light in, and allows the sociable homeowners to visit with neighbors strolling by.

▶ **The homeowner designed** this fresh take on the classic knot garden. Lettuces, marigolds, and bok choy take the place of carefully trained herbs to form an intricate pattern in the raised bed. A collapsible willow trellis rises from the center.

▲ **A built-in barbecue** is the star attraction in one of three concentric circular terraces.

▲ **Low cushion-topped seating walls** allow guests to relax in comfort while they kibitz with the cook.

▶ **A trickling fountain,** made from columnar basalt, forms the centerpiece of a second terrace.

▶ **Moss creeps** between Arizona flagstones, chosen for their soft, peachy-tan color.

▲ **A life-size baby giraffe,** christened Esmeralda, presides over an intimate seating area.

▼ **Watsonia, rockroses,** and 'Hot Lips' salvia peek through the fence.

▲ Before | With its cluttered walkway and pinched, generic front door, this entry was anything but welcoming.

Parthenocissus softens hard edges of the porch wall; its deep green foliage forms a rich counterpoint to the ocher color of the house.

Flagstones form a broad walkway and low walls around new flower beds. Their pale tone echoes the ivory trim on the house. Creeping thyme is planted between the flagstones, which are laid on sand and soil.

A fresh paint | After ▶ job, a new door with classic molding, and some simple landscaping changes add up to curbside savoir faire.

Containers of bower vine
(*Pandorea jasminoides*) flank
the garage door and begin
their climb over a new pergola.

A streetside bed of grevillea forms an
all-important focal point, drawing eyes
toward the now-attractive entryway.

▲ **Before** | The young couple who bought this house had never gardened before, but they'd perused enough pictures to know the look they wanted: formal structure combined with loose, even wild-looking plantings.

The homeowners called a landscape | **After** ▶ architect who drew up a plan calling for a variety of hardscape elements and a crazy-quilt mix of smaller trees, shrubs, perennials, and ornamental grasses.

Garden continues ▶ ▶

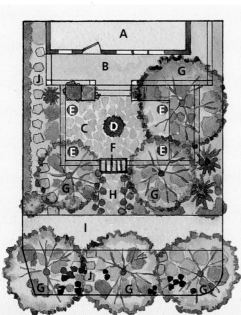

A House
B Porch
C Courtyard
D Urn
E Planters
F Arbor
G Trees at maturity
H Walkway
I Sidewalk
J Stepping stones

▲ **The homeowners built the arbor**—covered with golden hops (*Humulus lupulus* 'Aureus') and clematis (*Clematis jackmanii*)—which leads from the sidewalk to the courtyard. They also installed the low-voltage light system, thus leaving room in the budget for copper fixtures.

▶ **Four potted boxwood cones** surrounded by white-blooming 'Snowstorm' bacopa anchor the corners of the courtyard.

◀ **The new design** called for replacing two massive trees with smaller-scale varieties. A witch hazel, to the left of the arbor, and a purple-leaf smoke tree on the right add vertical interest without overwhelming the 35- by 22-foot plot.

▶ **Regal lilies** in a deep apricot shade bloom between low ground covers and a witch hazel (*Hamamelis mollis* 'Pallida').

▼ **Frothy bursts** of blue star creeper fill the gaps between stepping stones.

101

◀ Before | The owners of this house faced the same challenges that plague legions of their counterparts. Chief among them were noise and lack of privacy. (On both sides, neighboring homes almost touch the property line, and the lot fronts on a busy commuter road leading to a major city.) But the list went on: An asphalt driveway looked like a parking lot in front of the garage. To reach the house, pedestrians had to make their way over a narrow stone pathway that led from the street to the front door. Last but not least, there was just too much lawn to mow.

Now dense plantings all but block the street from view, and they've lowered the decibel level considerably. A wide walkway curves gracefully from the front steps to the resurfaced (and lower-key) driveway. And the only lawn is a tidy semicircle of grass the owners cut in minutes with a push mower.

After ▶

A large holly, left in place from the yard's previous incarnation, forms part of the garden's structural backbone. From certain angles, it also helps shield the large window.

▶ An exposed aggregate walkway, edged in Tennessee crab orchard stone, conveys residents and guests comfortably to the front door.

◄ **Vines climbing up an iron post** supply extra privacy at the front door, without closing it off so much that safety becomes a concern.

◄ **The yard spans just 35 feet** from the front door to the street. Largely for that reason, the owners chose not to build a fence. Instead, they opted for a living screen of carefully placed trees, shrubs, and perennials. Major players include azaleas, Japanese yews, doublefile viburnums, Leyland cypress, and a crabapple.

A rich mélange of perennials and ornamental grasses gives the owners plenty of opportunity to indulge their love of gardening. The roster includes verbena, Siberian iris, Oriental fountain grass, 'Blackie' sweet potato vine, 'Evergold' Japanese sedge, and 'Casa Blanca' lilies.

▲ **Before** | The young newlyweds who bought this house were thrilled with their first home—on the inside. The outside, with its bland-as-milk facade and long-neglected front yard, was another story. Unfortunately, the couple had a minuscule landscaping budget, limited time for outdoor work, and not a smidgen of gardening experience.

With help from | **After** ▶

a friend, the homeowners drew up a landscape plan, then rolled up their sleeves and got to work. The result: a charming, flower-filled entry garden that gave the sad little house a new lease on life.

Garden continues ▶ ▶

In a new garden, weeds pop up and spread at the speed of light. (At least it seems that way.) Inspect planting beds every day, or as often as you can, and pull out any invaders while they're still tiny. And do the job with your hands. If you use a weeding knife, rake, or other tool, you may damage the roots of young plants that you want to keep. There's also a good chance that you'll slice through the roots of perennial weeds, leaving pieces in the ground to multiply.

► **The woebegone entrance** cried out for help, but with a tight budget, building a new porch was out of the question.

The creative quick fix required only a couple buckets of paint, a packet of morning glory seeds, and a screwdriver to remove the old storm door.

Within a few weeks, the vines had scrambled up the railings and across the front of the overhang—helped along, the owners admit, by a lot of fertilizer (which, they now know, explains not only the oversized leaves, but also why these light eaters produced foliage galore but never bloomed). Still, the sunshine-yellow door did look lovely framed in deep green.

► **Crape myrtles,** planted on either side of the path leading from the driveway to the front door, help define and frame the walkway. Liriope, transplanted from the back yard, carpets the ground under the shrubs.

► **Many of the perennials,** including chrysanthemums, daylilies, gaura, and irises, began life in the gardens of family and friends. Now the owners treasure the plants for both their blooms and the memories they evoke.

106

◄ **Mother Nature** prompted the long-term solution. When frost killed the rampant morning glory vines, the couple opted for a slower, more lasting solution. They planted Carolina jessamine, an evergreen native to their southern territory, with fragrant yellow flowers in spring—and a far tidier growth habit than even underfed morning glories. They also found an attractive storm door at a flea market, painted it the same yellow as the inner door, and added a wire half-basket filled with vibrant annuals.

▼ **Pine straw mulch** (renewed once or twice a year) has given the beds a well-groomed look from day one. It also keeps roots cool, conserves moisture, and forms a barrier between the soil and wind-borne weed seeds. What's more, as it breaks down, it attracts beneficial organisms that improve the soil's structure.

▼ **A white picket fence,** purchased in prefab panels at a home center, performs several important functions in this garden. It gives structure to the scheme, helps tie the house to the landscape, and provides support for a rambling rose—the first plant the owners set into the ground.

▲ Before | This sliver of a balcony reflected the plight of many apartment and condo dwellers: no privacy, no character, and no ground whatsoever. The owner, an enthusiastic cook, longed for a garden where she could grow at least a few edibles to pluck "fresh from the vine."

What was nothing | After ▶ but an elevated concrete slab has become a bountiful garden brimming with fruits, vegetables, herbs, and cutting flowers. What's more, this potted paradise puts dinner makings only steps away from the kitchen and screens the view of, and from, neighboring units.

'Safari Pink' African daisies brighten up the railing.

Closely spaced containers of Spanish lavender top the second end wall, completely shielding the view from the next-door balcony.

Pots of thyme form a minihedge on the end wall.

A standard marguerite adds vertical interest, along with feathery foliage and cheery yellow blooms.

A chair and tiny table nestle among the plants, allowing the gardener to survey her domain from indoors or out.

▼ **A small stepladder,** retrofitted with boards on the bottom treads, holds 'Bright Lights' Swiss chard. Herbs and flowers soften the corner and blur the distinction between the balcony and the landscape beyond.

▲ **A console table** makes a clever (and space-enhancing) focal point at one end. Herbs and flowers crowd the shelves, drawers, and top. In floor-level pots, tomatoes, peppers, and a dwarf lemon stand ready for picking.

109

This **Before** ▶ lot appears to slope gently downhill. In fact, the land drops a full 12 feet from the front of the house to the Potomac River behind it. The soil is heavy marine clay—a nightmare-come-true for most garden plants. But that dual design challenge was a piece of cake compared with the homeowners' major concern: From time to time, the river leaps its banks and floodwater sweeps across the lawn.

▼ **After** | The owners called in a garden designer, who employed a classic, two-part strategy: He reshaped the site into a series of terraces and chose a palette of plants that can handle both heavy soil and periodic flooding. The lawn was raised several feet at its lower end and sodded with a mixture of fine-leafed fescues. The grass can handle brief immersion in floodwater and the pelting debris that comes with it. A low stone wall separates the lawn from the riverbank, where the designer chose plants that mimic "a wild, wet meadow."

Garden continues ▶ ▶

▲ **Out of sight** beneath the black umbrella, a small deck provides ringside seats for the ever-changing show on the river. A wooden walkway, also hidden by the vegetation, connects the structure to the lawn.

▲ **Broad sweeps of switch grass** (*Panicum virgatum* 'Heavy Metal') fill the space between the wall and the river's riprap edge. Besides giving the scene a silvery glow and holding the fragile soil in place, the switch grass absorbs nutrient runoff from the lawn before it reaches the water. Much to the owners' delight, the planting also deters that bane of shoreside property owners, Canada geese—at least so far.

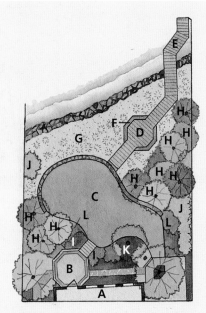

A House
B Patio and steps
C Lawn
D Wood deck
E Dock
F Wood seat
G Switch grass
H Magnolia
I Bayberry
J Wax myrtle
K Dogwood
L Rugosa rose

▶ **Framed by two boat docks** (a neighbor's on the right; the owners' on the left), a young Kousa dogwood lends vertical interest to the composition.

▶ *Lysimachia* **and** *Rudbeckia laciniata* lend height and flashes of color to the flat waterscape.

▶ **A stone wall** rims a walkway leading from the bottom of the driveway to the back door.

▶ **Pink lantana, pink rugosa roses,** and the burgundy foliage of 'Crimson Pigmy' barberry soften the wall's sharp angles.

◄ **A flight of stairs** leads from a seating area to the newly lowered lawn (just visible beyond the switch grass). Petunias in ceramic pots provide bright color and sweet fragrance all summer long.

▼ **Before:** At the side of the house, a steep driveway ended abruptly at a lawn that, to put it mildly, did nothing to enhance the river view.

Who among us wouldn't love to have a place with a knock-your-socks-off view? The fact is, though, that gardening in the shadow of a gorgeous vista has its challenges, both aesthetic and practical. Here's a trio of tips on making the most of a good thing.

■ When you're faced with a difficult environment (as dramatic terrain tends to be), think big. Plants in 1-gallon containers will get off to a faster start and, therefore, stand a better chance of survival than do less mature specimens.

■ Don't try to compete with Mother Nature. If you're blessed with a beautiful view, keep the foreground simple. Keep eyes focused on the star attraction by using broad swathes of a single type of plant, such as the switch grass used here.

■ Confine complexity to areas close to the house. And even then, take a low-key approach. For instance, stick to a single flower color (or maybe two), but vary foliage texture.

◄ Before

With its meandering stone walkways, hulking boulders, and dark facade, this place was singin' the grays. And the fact that massive oak trees (out of sight in this picture) kept the yard in constant shade didn't help matters any. The homeowners wanted a warmer, lighter, more welcoming entryway that would double as usable outdoor space.

The welcome mat is out, thanks | ## After ▶
to a few simple changes. On the advice of a designer, the owners pruned the oaks to let in more sun, repainted the house a light golden tan, and replaced the stone paths and struggling vegetation with broad walkways and a few choice plants.

▶ **Handmade pots,** purchased locally, pick up the orangey-tan shades of the stone walls. The contents change with the seasons, but the color range remains the same green and white, as in the calla lilies and lamium shown here.

▲ **Masses of heavenly bamboo** and bright pink azaleas replaced the scruffy ferns and scraggly shrubs.

A sculpture by a local artist sets a personal tone and marks the turn toward the doorway.

Low, broad walls of Bouquet Canyon stone define the paved space and provide ample seating for outdoor gatherings. Lights set into the ends illuminate the scene at night.

Straight lines of *Liriope muscari* edge the walkway, guiding the eye toward the entrance.

▲ **A tan-tinted walkway**—broad enough to serve as a patio—leads directly to the porch and a new, brightly painted door.

115

Before | A major remodeling had turned this from a nice-enough house to the owners' dream home, with all the charm and quirky angles of cottages they'd admired on treks through the French countryside. Make that almost all the charm. Those bare walls were sorely lacking in pizazz.

A few simple details | **After ▶** did the trick. Like the house itself, the plantings evoke a rural European feeling, but for the wife—a *trompe l'oeil* painter—this was a case of life imitating art. For years she had painted eye-fooling window boxes, urns, and vines on other people's walls. Now, she decked her own place with the real things.

Garden continues ▶ ▶

◀ **The formerly unadorned window** above the garage now sports wire-brushed wooden shutters stained to match the frame. The homeowner plied her trade on the window box, painting the new wood to look old and mellow. Then she filled it with an informal arrangement of ivy, blue bacopa, yellow ranunculus, magenta geraniums, and pink tulips.

▲ **Before:** Despite its soothing curves, the entryway offered a pretty bleak welcome before its new look.

▶ **Now, copies of antique French urns** flank the door. The boxwood topiaries remain year-round, but the flowers at their "feet" change with the seasons. Here, in spring, the cast includes white bacopa, blue campanula, and peach-toned tulips.

◀ **The homeowners had this folk-art bird-house** tucked away for years. Now, they thought, might be the time to pull it out of retirement. Their hunch was right. Tucked into a corner, the rustic little structure provides a perfect complement to the sturdy corbel and wood-framed casement window. A white, spring-flowering clematis climbs the post; a blue hydrangea cloaks the bottom.

Evergreen shrubs such as *Ceanothus thyrsiflorus* 'Victoria' and *Viburnum davidii* provide both year-round structure and seasonal bursts of color (blue spring flowers in the case of *Ceanothus;* white blooms on the *Viburnum*).

The garden owes its on-going good looks to striking foliage plants, including *Senecio greyi* 'Sunshine', blue oat grass, variegated Japanese sedge, and 'Apricot Beauty' phormium.

◀ **Before** | From some angles, this overgrown wisteria appeared poised to conquer the neighborhood. As for the lawn, besides looking boring at best, it consumed far more water than the homeowner cared to provide.

◀ **After** | Now a vibrant tapestry of perennials, grasses, and shrubs literally stops traffic. What's more, the plants look great all year around, and thrive on half the water the old lawn required.

◀ **Using a rented sod cutter,** the homeowner stripped off all but a few curving paths of grass. She tilled a 6-inch layer of planting mix (a commercial blend of compost, ground bark, peat moss, and sand) into the soil, then planted closely spaced sweeps of perennials and shrubs.

▼ **A savvy choice of perennials** ensures vibrant blooms from spring through fall. This *Aster × frikartii* produces lavender, daisylike flowers starting in early summer.

◀ Before | This jumble of plants, cracked concrete, and assorted debris greeted the new tenant of a house in San Francisco. Like many renters, he did his best to ignore the scene for several years. Finally, though, a lifelong passion for gardening and a craving for an outdoor sanctuary spurred him to action (and, a few years later, into buying the house). An interior designer by profession, he knew the importance of setting both aesthetic and practical goals, and he was crystal clear on both counts: he wanted a space with an aura of spirituality and a roster of "bullet-proof" plants.

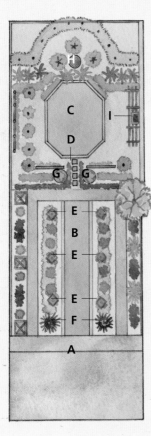

A House and patio
B Lower lawn
C Upper lawn
D Stairs
E Standard 'Iceberg' roses
F New Zealand flax
G 'Flutterbye' roses and 'Skyrocket' juniper
H Urn on pillar
I Wall fountain

He laid out a series | After ▶ of formal, symmetrical spaces and then filled them with a carefully choreographed cast of rugged, low-maintenance plants—including several retained from the original yard and propagated from cuttings. The garden evoked exactly the sort of meditative atmosphere he wanted. What he didn't realize, until visitors began pointing it out, was that his design precisely mimics the floor plan of a church.

Garden continues ▶ ▶

For the lawn, the owner chose the most drought-tolerant seed mix his local nursery had to offer.

▼ **Each of the six 'Iceberg' roses** in the long borders stands in a planter made from square concrete blocks, stacked four high. The underplantings change with the seasons, but the half-dozen groupings always match. Here the inventory (chosen for its red, purple, and yellow color scheme) consists of Swiss chard, California poppies, red-and yellow-leafed geraniums (*Pelargonium* × *hortorum* 'Vancouver'), and purple violas.

▲ **A weathered concrete path,** retained from the original garden, borders the lower rectangle.

◀ **Italian buckthorn** forms a dense screen behind a plant-filled urn, set on a pillar and surrounded by three eucalyptus trees.

◀ **At the entrance** to the upper garden, hedges of rosemary (grown from cuttings of a plant found in the original garden) wrap around pots of 'Flutterbye' roses interplanted with 'Skyrocket' juniper.

◀ **Identically planted borders** flank the lower lawn. The permanent residents are New Zealand flax, standard 'Iceberg' roses, Mexican sage, yellow nasturtiums, and 'Stella d'Oro' daylilies. Trex® boards, salvaged from a construction-site rubble heap, edge the beds.

▶ **Grapes and climbing 'Westerland' roses** cloak a neighbor's concrete-block wall. The rose's blooms echo the colors of the 'Flutterbyes' flanking the stairs.

▶ **This "venerable" terra-cotta fountain** is actually a brand new, cast-acrylic model, treated with a coat of concrete stain. Hanging oil lamps cast a soft glow on the wall at night.

◀ **New Zealand flax** shares a pot with hens and chicks. Around it, planted in the ground, are yellow nasturtiums, sedge, and 'Stella d'Oro' daylilies (not yet in bloom).

◀ **A French urn** sits on a pillar made from concrete blocks stained a matching terra-cotta color. Inside the pot, New Zealand flax, agave, and variegated African daisies mingle happily.

DESIGN TIP

At first glance, the presence of large container plants in this garden seems at odds with the owner's desire for a low-maintenance, water-thrifty landscape. On the contrary, they help him achieve that goal. How so? They're bottomless—thereby forcing the plants' roots to grow downward into deep, moisture-holding levels of the soil. To open up the terra-cotta pots, he simply turned each one over on its top (using a thick towel to cushion the edge), inserted a pair of broad pliers into the drainage hole, and carefully broke off pieces of clay until only an inch or two of lip remained around the sides. Then he sunk the pot an inch or two into the ground, and installed the plants.

Installing Sod

One of the quickest garden makeovers you can do is simply to lay down new sod. It takes some prior planning and shopping, but a small to average-size area can be installed in a day.

Gather Your Gear

Determine the best turf grass for your site, find a reliable supplier, and order sod for delivery on the morning of planting day. This garden took 16 rolls. Order a roll or two more than you think you'll need, so you don't come up short.

Call a rental yard and reserve a sod roller and rear-tined rotary tiller for pickup early on planting day. (Whatever you do, don't use a tiller with the tines in front; they're all but impossible to control.)

Before planting day, you'll also need a garden hose with a sprinkler head, a sharp knife, a rake, and a shovel.

Getting Started

If the soil in your future garden is good loam, you'll want to spread a 1-inch layer of compost over the entire area. For soil that's high in either sand or clay, plan on 2 inches. Because compost is usually sold by the cubic yard, you'll need to do some calculating before you head to the garden center. Here's the basic equation: 3 cubic yards of compost = 1-inch layer per 1,000 square feet. (Always feel free to round up—it's impossible to overdose on compost.)

1 **After spreading the compost** evenly across the surface, till the soil to a depth of at least 8 inches. Then level the ground and rake it to remove large stones and other debris.

2 **Spread flour, sand, or powdered gypsum** on the ground to outline the lawn area. (Or, if you prefer, lay down a light-colored rope to mark the space.)

3 **Lay the sod strips** on top of the soil, in a staggered bond pattern, so the joints of one row fall in the middle of solid strips on either side. Take care to push the edges tightly together. Trim the outer edges with a sharp knife to fit the outline.

4 **Push the roller** (filled halfway with water) over the sod to press its root zone into firm contact with the soil.

5 **When you've finished planting**, water the beds and lawn. Later, for a finished look and to make mowing easier, you can edge the beds with flagstone or bricks (cut out chunks of sod to accommodate the stones). Finally, add comfortable seating or some outdoor art. We opted for both in the form of a hand-carved wooden bench.

For the first month or so after you install your sod, water every morning until the soil is soaked 6 to 8 inches below the surface. Also, to ensure the strongest crop of turf, stay off the grass as much as possible for 4 to 6 weeks (or until you can't lift the corners of the strips.)

127

127

▲ Before | This place had been

home for more than two decades. The owners loved the house—and the view—as much as ever, but the garden was another story. They weren't quite sure what they wanted in its place, but they knew for certain what they didn't want. For starters, the thirsty grass had to go. So did the line of junipers that separated the lawn from an almost-vertical drop. Of course, they'd still need some sort of plants to hold the ground in place. For that job they wanted… Well, the designer they hired could make that decision.

And she did. She chose a ## After ▶

variety of deep-rooted, dry-climate natives that anchor the soil, highlight the breathtaking vista, and prevent anyone from tumbling over the edge. But she did more than that. She turned the yard's bland expanse into an extension of the home's interior—a multihued, multitextured mélange that reflects the owners' light-hearted personalities.

Garden continues ▶ ▶

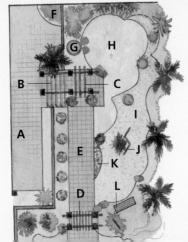

A Upper patio

B Stairs

C Arbor with wisteria

D Entrance arbor

E Tile walkway

F Fireplace

G Water feature

H New concrete patio

I Salmon Bay gravel
   bed

J Screen

K Mosaic tile

L Bench

▲ **A tinted concrete patio,** extending from the existing tile walkway, replaced part of the lawn.

▲ **Salmon Bay gravel** fills the space between the patio and the abrupt drop-off. In bright sunlight, its soft, sandy beige tones reflect less glare than gray stones would.

130

In any successful design, repetition plays a key role, and this garden presents a stunning case in point. For example, round shapes appear over and over, in pots, mounding plants, and even the curved sections of the new patio. The same mosaic-tile trim accents a wall, forms a section of the patio, and outlines the fireplace. In turn, the tile's blue and terra-cotta tones are reprised in floors, walls, and pots throughout the landscape.

◀ **The designer found this rusted steel screen** at a Mexican import shop, set it near the edge of the cliff, and anchored it with lengths of rebar driven three feet into the soil. The panel serves the practical purpose of blocking some of the wind that sweeps up from below, but part of its job is purely aesthetic: The designer feels that to deliver maximum impact, a dramatic view needs to be partitioned at some point.

◀ **A potted palm,** underplanted with white bacopa, helps reinforce the screen. Palm-and-bacopa pairings recur throughout the garden.

▶ **At one end of the house,** the tile walkway expands to form a terrace, complete with a fireplace and (out of sight) a barbecue grill. In the original scheme, the wall and fireplace were pale beige; the designer painted them a rich terra-cotta and added the mosaic tile border around the firebox.

This place could have won a "Neighborhood's Most | Before ▶

Boring Yard" contest hands down, but the owner couldn't have cared less. Then one day, on a whim, she decided to take out the juniper that stretched across the front of the house and replace it with "something more interesting."

◄ After │ She enjoyed the result so much, she just kept going. Now, six years later, a mind-boggling assortment of trees, shrubs, annuals, and perennials fills the former lawn and the 10-foot-deep parking strip. Thanks to careful plant selection and a mild climate, the colorful display goes on year-round. The homeowner terms her creation a "disciplined cottage garden." Her neighbors call it "a gift to the neighborhood."

Garden continues ▶ ▶

▲ **Before:** Shortly after banishing the junipers, the homeowner planted a couple of upright Japanese maples to accompany the mounding, red-leafed one already on the scene. Then she tucked a 'Victoria' ceanothus (the burgundy-leafed plant) into the corner by the porch and added a bed of colorful annuals.

▲ The *Ceanothus* completely hides the porch. Sharing its quarters are *Cerinthe major*, *Diascia*, wallflower, and a 'Lavender Pinocchio' rose.

▲ **In front of the house,** a fieldstone terrace surrounds two of the pioneer maples.

▲ **Stone walkways** enclose a triangular bed holding one of the original maples, now joined by *Tradescantia*, catmint, blue star creeper, and *Diascia*.

▲ **Before:** The back yard offered the luxury of total enclosure, but had little else going for it.

▼ **A 9- by 12-foot pond,** stocked with a thriving population of goldfish, forms the centerpiece of the new backyard garden.

▼ **Stepping stones** near the "shore" rest on soil but the center one, which appears to be floating, is mortared to a pedestal, which in turn is mortared to the pond's flexible liner.

▼ **A hollowed-out boulder** serves as a birdbath. (Winged visitors also enjoy splashing in the shallow end of the pond.)

▼ **A carpet of gold-toned Scotch moss** (*Sagina subulata* 'Aurea') has replaced the old lawn.

▼ **Foliage in a multitude of forms,** textures, and colors ensures year-round interest. Plants include euphorbia, hebe, wallflower, corydalis, roses, and butterfly bush.

DESIGN TIP

Design professionals constantly talk about striving for "a long season of interest" in a garden. That might sound like a complex undertaking, but it's really quite simple. For starters, try some—or all—of these tricks.

■ Plant spring bulbs among later-emerging perennials. For instance, group daffodils with hostas or tulips with astilbe.

■ Train a late-flowering vine to grow through the branches of an earlier-blooming shrub. Clematis and roses are a classic combo.

■ Choose deciduous trees and shrubs that have dramatic branching patterns, distinctive bark, or colorful berries, as well as eye-catching flowers and foliage. There are many; your best options depend on where you live, but four-season superstars include golden-twig dogwood, buttercup winter hazel, rockspray cotoneaster (*C. microphyllus*), and Russian olive.

■ Seek out flowering perennials with beautiful form and foliage. Peonies, cranesbill, daylilies, astilbe, and blue false indigo are easy-to-grow favorites.

■ Grow plenty of flowering annuals in containers (or buy them when the need arises) and whisk them into place to fill bare spots or mask the withering leaves of spring bulbs. The sky's the limit here!

▲ Before | This sunny, south-facing plot yielded bumper vegetable harvests, but its long, narrow shape presented two problems: It limited the range of crops (and therefore production) and made plant-tending awkward. Furthermore, the garden did nothing to enhance the appearance of the side yard it occupied.

The simple solution: Divide | **After ▶** and conquer. Five smaller beds, separated by 2-foot-wide gravel paths, allow easy access for planting, weeding, and harvesting. Containers and vertical supports provide homes for a wider variety of edibles, while giving the design important structural "bones."

The tall hedge of creeping fig does triple duty in this narrow garden: It blocks the wind, forms a unifying backdrop for more colorful plants, and hides a prosaic wall of concrete block.

Perennial plants such as artichokes, rosemary, and thyme keep beds looking good almost all year, while also yielding a harvest.

Matching terra-cotta bowls at the front of each bed are planted with herbs, alpine strawberries, and edible flowers.

▶ A bent-willow teepee and a Texas Tornado tomato cage provide vertical interest in a bed of low-growing herbs and keep sprawling plants in line.

Redwood header boards outline each bed; paths between beds are covered with Del Rio gravel that complements the stone walkway.

▲Before

Like most urbanites, the new owner of this big-city house longed for a quiet, private space where she could entertain friends on balmy evenings, read quietly, or simply wind down with a glass of wine after a long day at work. What she had was a dysfunctional mishmash of precast pavers, plain concrete, and oddly shaped planting beds—bounded by two garages and a four-story apartment building.

After▶

The homeowner called in a design duo who quickly turned the collection of eyesores into a city-dweller's dream: a sophisticated, comfortable, and low-maintenance retreat.

Garden continues ▶ ▶

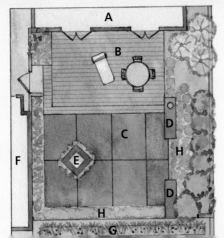

A House

B Deck

C Patio

D Benches

E Water feature

F Garage

G Bamboo screening
apartment building

H Raised beds made
from salvaged pavers
and concrete

Timber bamboo softens a cinder block wall and screens the apartment building rising above it.

The raised beds are made from the garden's original concrete floor, cut into strips and sandwiched with the precast pavers.

▲ **A concrete patio,** scored into square sections, complements the straight-lined geometry of both house and garden. Its rich, blue-violet color teams with masses of deep green foliage and a few white accents to create instant relief from sensory overload.

▲ **A small, square pool** echoes the shape and color of the patio segments.

▼ **The broad, low deck,** made from sustainably harvested hardwood, performs a dual function. One is obvious: It provides an attractive space for dining or relaxing, just steps from the kitchen. On a more serious note, the raised platform allowed the designers to resolve a persistent drainage problem, while keeping the hardware out of sight.

▼ **An assortment** of dense, mostly evergreen foliage plants disguises a garage wall and helps muffle noise.

▲ **Benches,** in the same wood used for the deck, carry its color, texture, and lines into the garden—as well as providing extra seating for guests.

▶ **This simple, unplumbed water feature** serves as a sort of visual mantra, guiding the viewer's thoughts away from external hubbub, and inward toward petals floating in a glass-tiled bowl.

Design and Photography Credits

DESIGN

6–7 Tom Mannion 8–11 Tom Mannion 12–13 Jeffrey Gordon Smith 14–17 Jeff Bale 18–19 Consulting Designer: Neil Odenwald 20–23 Landscape Architect: Tom Keithe 24–25 Élan Landscape Design & Build 30–31 Gay Bonorden Gray 32–35 Conni Cross 36–37 Tyler Gerdes 38–41 Nicholas Walker, Jardin du Jour; Craig Prunty and Mario Navarro, All Oregon Landscaping; Barbara Butler Artist-Builder (playhouse) 44–45 Tom Mannion 46–49 Shari Bashin-Sullivan, Enchanting Planting 50–51 Tom Mannion 52–55 Tom Mannion 56–57 Cal Native Landscaping 58–61 Conni Cross 64–65 Anne Janisse, City People's Gardens Design & Landscape; Fence: Jim Paulsen 66–69 Designers: Rochelle Ford and Richard Wogisch 70–71 Tom Mannion 72–75 Paul Fitzgerald, Polyscapes.com 76–77 Chuck Rathfon 78 Jim Ripley 79 Philip Edinger 80–83 Cathy Hoekman, Concept Landscapes, Inc. 86–89 Goodman Landscape Design 90–91 Paul Robbins 92–95 KT Foust, Flor Garden Habitats 96–97 John Williams Design 98–101 David Pfeiffer, Garden Architecture Inc. 102–103 Tom Mannion 104–107 Tina Cornett 108–109 Jill Slater 110–113 Tom Mannion 114–115 Jessy Berg, APLD, Berg Designs 120–121 Stacie Crooks, Crooks Garden Design 122–125 Randall Holman 126–127 Bud Stuckey 128–131 Bonnie McGregor, McGregor Design Studio 132–135 Darcy Daniels, Bloomtown Garden Design & Nursery 136–137 Lew Whitney, Roger's Gardens 138–141 Matthew Henning and Heather Anderson, Henning–Anderson.

PHOTOGRAPHY

Before Marion Brenner: 108; Tina Cornett: 104; Darcy Daniels: 133, 134, 135; Roger Foley: 6, 44, 50, 53, 70, 110; Tyler Gerdes: 36; Cathy Hoekman: 80, 82; Randall Holman: 122; Tom Mannion: 8, 102; Jim McCausland: 120; John Paulsen: 64; Allen Rokach/SPC: 84; Susan A. Roth: 33, 35, 58, 60.

After Scott Atkinson: 79; Ted Betz: 87–89; Marion Brenner: 108–109; Van Chaplin/SPC: 18–19, 20–23, 26–29, 42; Ken Chen: 76–77, 96; Connie Coleman: 64–65; Tina Cornett/SPC: 104–107; Claire Curran: 136–137; Andrew Drake: 98–101; Roger Foley: 6, 8–11, 44–45, 50, 52–55, 70, 110–113; Frank Gaglione; 56–57, 66–69, 72–75, 92–95, 114–115, 116–119, 123–125, 128–131; Steven Gunther: 12, 90; Saxon Holt: 46–49, 78; Janet Loughrey: 38–41, 132–135; Allan Mandell: 14–17, 80–83; Sylvia Martin/SPC: 102–103; Jim McCausland: 121; Norman A. Plate: 43, 62–63, 126; Norm Plate: 36, 120, 138–141; Allen Rokach/SPC: 84; Susan A. Roth: 32–35, 58–61; Thomas J. Story: 30, 127; Ben Woolsey: 24–25.

Index